Homilies from the Heart

YEAR A

Msgr. Robert D. Fuller

Published by
KAN Distributing Inc.

Copyright 2009, Msgr. Robert D. Fuller

All rights reserved. No part of this publication may be reproduced, stored in a retrieval system, or transmitted in any form or by any means—electronic, mechanical, photocopy, recording, or any other—except for brief quotations in printed reviews, without the prior permission of the publisher.

Biblical citation abbreviations are consistent with The Chicago Manual of Style, 14th Edition, 1993.

The Book Team:
Ernie Nedder, Publisher
Kathy Nedder, CFO
Msgr. Robert D. Fuller, Author
Sharon Nicks of Types, Graphic Design

Printed in the United States
KAN Distributing

Individual Copies: $12.00

Ordering Information
Check local bookstores
From the author: 520-326-7670
or email: cabrini1962@aol.com
Order #KAN1606

ISBN: 978-09841716-0-6

DEDICATION

This book is dedicated in gratitude to God for the wonderful vocation of priesthood, to my family, to Adolfo Quezada and Katherine Smith, who made this book possible, and to all the loving people who have encouraged me through the years.

Msgr. Robert D. Fuller

Any profit from this book will be donated to the Catholic Worker House, Casa Maria, in Tucson, Arizona

TABLE OF CONTENTS

Foreword
Most Reverend Gerald F. Kicanas, D.D. 1

Preface 3

FIRST SUNDAY OF ADVENT
(Is 2:1-5; Rom 13:11-14; Mt 24:37-44) 5

SECOND SUNDAY OF ADVENT
(Is 11:1-10; Rom 15:4-9; Mt 3:1-12) 9

THIRD SUNDAY OF ADVENT
(Is 35:1-6, 10; Jas 5:7-10; Mt 11:2-11) 12

FOURTH SUNDAY OF ADVENT
(Is 7:10-14; Rom 1:1-7; Mt 1:18-24) 15

CHRISTMAS
(Is 9:1-6; Ti 2:11-14; Lk 2:1-14) 18

HOLY FAMILY
(Sir 3:2-7, 12-14; Col 3:12-21; Mt 2:13-15, 19-23) 21

EPIPHANY
(Is 60:1-6; Eph 3:2-3a, 5-6; Mt 2:1-12) 24

BAPTISM OF JESUS
(Is 42:1-4, 6-7; Acts 10:34-38; Mt 3:13-17) 28

SECOND SUNDAY OF THE YEAR
(Is 49:3, 5-6; 1 Cor 1:1-3; Jn 1:29-34) 31

THIRD SUNDAY OF THE YEAR
(Is 8:23-9:3; 1 Cor 1:10-13, 17; Mt 4:12-23) 34

Fourth Sunday of the Year
(Zep 2:3; 3:12-13; 1Cor 1:26-31; Mt 5:1-12a) 37

Fifth Sunday of the Year
(Is 58:7-10; 1 Cor 2:1-5; Mt 5:13-16) 40

First Sunday of Lent
(Gn 2:7-9, 3:17; Rom 5:12-19; Mt 4:1-11) 43

Second Sunday of Lent
(Gn 12:1-4a; 2 Tim 1:8b-10; Mt 17:1-9) 47

Third Sunday of Lent
(Ex 17:3-7; Rom 5:1-2, 5-8; Jn 4:5-42) 51

Fourth Sunday of Lent
(1 Sam 16:1b, 6-7, 10-13a; Eph 5:8-14; Jn 9: 1-41) 54

Fifth Sunday of Lent
(Ezek 37:12-14; Rom 8: 8-11; Jn 11: 1-45) 57

Palm (Passion) Sunday
(Is 50:4-7; Phil 2:6-11; Mt 26:14-27, 66) 59

Holy Thursday
(Ex 12:1-8, 11-14; 1 Cor 11:23-26; Jn 13:1-15) 61

Good Friday
(Is 52:13-53:12; Heb 4:14-16, 5:7-9; Jn 18:1-19:42) 64

Easter Sunday
(Acts 10:34a, 37-43; Col 3:1-4; Jn 20:1-9) 67

Second Sunday of Easter
(Acts 2:42-47; 1 Pt 1:3:9; Jn 20:19-31) 69

Third Sunday of Easter
(Acts 2:14, 22-33; 1 Pt 1:17-21; Lk 24:13-35) 72

FOURTH SUNDAY OF EASTER
(Acts 2:14a, 36-41; 1 Pt 2:20b-25; Jn 10:1-10) 75

FIFTH SUNDAY OF EASTER
(Acts 6:1-7; 1 Pt 2:4-9; Jn 14:1-12) 79

SIXTH SUNDAY OF EASTER
(Acts 8:5-8, 14-17; 1Pt 3:15-18; Jn 14:15-21) 82

SEVENTH SUNDAY OF EASTER
(Acts 1:12-14; 1 Pt 4:13-16; Jn 17:1-11a) 85

ASCENSION
(Acts 1:1-11; Eph 1:17-23; Mt 28:16-20) 88

PENTECOST
(Acts 2:1-11; 1 Cor 12:3b-7, 12-13; Jn 20:19-23) 91

TRINITY SUNDAY
(Ex 34:4b-6; 2 Cor 13:11-13; Jn 3) 94

CORPUS CHRISTI
(Dt 8:2-3, 14b-16a; 1 Cor 10:16-17; Jn 6:51-58) 97

TENTH SUNDAY OF THE YEAR
(Hos 6:3-6; Rom 4:18-25; Mt 9:9-13) 100

ELEVENTH SUNDAY OF THE YEAR
(Ex 19:2-6a; Rom 5:6-11; Mt 9:36-10:8) 103

TWELFTH SUNDAY OF THE YEAR
(Jer 20:10-13; Rom 5:12-15; Mt 10: 26-33) 106

THIRTEENTH SUNDAY OF THE YEAR
(2 Kgs 4:8-11, 14-16a; Rom 3:6-4, 8-11; Mt 10:37-42) 109

FOURTEENTH SUNDAY OF THE YEAR
(Zec 9:9-10; Rom 8:9, 11-13; Mt 11:25-30) 112

FIFTEENTH SUNDAY OF THE YEAR
(Is 55:10-11; Rom 8:18-23; Mt 13:1-9) 116

SIXTEENTH SUNDAY OF THE YEAR
(Wis 12:13, 16-19; Rom 8:26-27; Mt 13:24-30) 119

SEVENTEENTH SUNDAY OF THE YEAR
(1 Kgs 3:5, 7-12; Rom 8:28-30; Mt 13:44-46) 122

EIGHTEENTH SUNDAY OF THE YEAR
(Is 55:1-3; Rom 8:35, 37-39; Mt 14:13-21) 125

NINETEENTH SUNDAY OF THE YEAR
(1 Kgs 14:9a,11-13a; Rom 9:1-5; Mt 14:22-33) 129

TWENTIETH SUNDAY OF THE YEAR
(Is 96:1, 6-7; Rom 11:13-15, 24-32; Mt 15:21-28) 132

TWENTY-FIRST SUNDAY OF THE YEAR
(Is 22:19-26; Rom 11:33-36; Mt 16:13-20) 135

TWENTY-SECOND SUNDAY OF THE YEAR
(Jer 20:7-9; Rom 12:1-2; Mt 16:21-27) 139

TWENTY-THIRD SUNDAY OF THE YEAR
(Ez 33:7-9; Rom 13:8-10; Mt 18:15-20) 142

TWENTY-FOURTH SUNDAY OF THE YEAR
(Sir 27:30-28:9; Rom 14:7-9; Mt 18:21-35) 145

TWENTY-FIFTH SUNDAY OF THE YEAR
(Is 55:6-9; Phil 1:20c-24, 27a; Mt 20:1-16a) 149

TWENTY-SIXTH SUNDAY OF THE YEAR
(Ez 18:25-28; Phil 2:1-11; Mt 21:28-32) 152

TWENTY-SEVENTH SUNDAY OF THE YEAR
(Is 5:1-7; Phil 4:6-9; Mt 21:33-43) 156

Twenty-Eighth Sunday of the Year
(Is 25:6-10a; Phil 4:12-14, 19-20; Mt 22:1-10) 159

Twenty-Ninth Sunday of the Year
(Is 45:1, 4-6; 1 Thes 1:1-5b; Mt 22:15-21) 162

Thirtieth Sunday of the Year
(Ex 22:20-26; 1 Thes 1:5c-10; Mt 22:34-40) 165

Thirty-First Sunday of the Year
(Mal 1:14-2:2b, 8-10; 1 Thes 2:7b-9,13; Mt 23:1-12) 168

Thirty-Second Sunday of the Year
(Wis 6:12-16; 1 Tes 4:13-18; Mt 25:1-3) 171

Thirty-Third Sunday of the Year
(Prov 31:10-13, 19020, 30-31; 1 Thes 5:1-6; Mt 25:14-38) . 174

Christ the King
(Ez 34:11-12, 15-17; 1 Cor 15:20-26, 28; Mt 25:31-46) 177

FOREWORD

In a culture and society filled with mass media and advanced methods of communicating you might think that preaching is outdated, passé, no longer relevant. But when you talk to people in a parish community, where a priest preaches well every Sunday, you realize preaching remains important. God's word preached with passion and conviction still matters, still touches people in significant ways by moving hearts and even transforming lives.

Monsignor Robert D. Fuller, a priest of the Diocese of Tucson, is such a preacher.

Always prepared, he breaks open God's Word in a way that stirs hearts and deepens hunger for the Lord. Monsignor Fuller speaks in concrete language, uses human experience, and always remains faithful to the scriptural text. He makes a bishop proud.

Many research studies have revealed the hunger people have for good preaching. They want homilies that are spiritual, thoughtful, meaningful, and that move them into a closer relationship with God. *Homilies from the Heart* contains such homilies. Over the liturgical year, Monsignor Fuller uses a variety of ways to lead people into deeper contact with the scriptures.

The people of St. Frances Cabrini Parish brag about his homilies, delight in them, and are fed by them. As you read *Homilies from the Heart*, you will see why his people consider themselves blessed.

These homilies will provide preachers with much food for thought and will provide homiletic teachers with good examples of what preaching can and should be. The spiritual messages found in this book will inspire you and stay with you!

> Most Reverend Gerald F. Kicanas, D.D.
> *Bishop of Tucson*

PREFACE

When American Catholics are surveyed, one of their biggest complaints is that the preaching they hear in church is not good. I take this seriously because our weekend liturgies are the best opportunity we have to communicate God's Word to our faith communities. When I say that I take this seriously, I mean I work hard to give the best I have, as imperfect as it may be. I keep working at it, and when I receive positive feedback I thank God because, as an introvert, public speaking does not come easy to me.

This book is not intended to be another of the many prepared-homily services that are available to priests. If there is a fellow-priest or deacon who finds my homilies helpful in the preparation of his own homilies, I will be pleased and honored that my words can be useful in this way. But this book is written for anyone who finds it a helpful companion on their spiritual journey.

As I often tell my own parish community, the homilies I write are for my benefit as well as theirs. I often need to hear what my parishioners need to hear because we are all confronted with the same human condition. In my homilies I use the pronoun "we" instead of "you," because I am preaching to myself as well.

These homilies are brief and to the point, and the theme that runs through them is love. A well-known South American priest and retreat master, Fr. Mateo, wrote, "If I have convinced one person that God really loves him or her then my life has been worthwhile." I feel the same about my parish community and now, about you, the reader.

Msgr. Robert D. Fuller
July 27, 2009

📖 First Sunday of Advent
(Is 2:1-5; Rom 13:11-14; Mt 24:37- 44)

It is the First Sunday of Advent. Advent comes from the Latin word that means "coming." It is a special time to prepare ourselves for the coming of Jesus at Christmas and the coming of Jesus at the end of our life.

Shortly before President John F. Kennedy's fateful trip to Dallas, his secretary found a note he had written by hand. It read, "I know there is a God and I see a storm coming. If he has a place for me, I believe that I am ready." How about us? How shall we be ready? Let's take our cue from the second reading and from today's Gospel. Paul urges us to be prepared. "It is the hour now for you to awake from sleep." In our Gospel, Jesus urges us the same way, "You must be prepared. Therefore, stay awake."

Let's make this our theme for Advent, to awaken from sleep and stay awake. But what kind of "awake" are we talking about? Awake to what? A mother gives us a hint when she writes about her three-year-old daughter, Alexia. She would wake up each morning with a joyful shout, "I wake up to the morning!" Now we adults might say, "Of course she did. We all wake up in the morning." But this is not the point. Alexia was delighted at seeing that the sun had risen again. It made another morning and what we adults take for granted, was extraordinary for her.

Full of energy, Alexia would leap out of bed ready for the new day. She was awake to life. We tend to go through life half-asleep and unaware of the world around us and the world within us. How do we know if we are awake to life or half asleep? When we are half-asleep life becomes strictly routine, just as series of tasks and obligations that make us feel trapped and burdened. We become creatures of habit and our habits box us in and stifle our spirit. We may wake up with the sun but we have lost our sense of wonder and excitement. If we can identify with this, then we are not yet awake to life.

Fr. Bernard Lonergan said the same thing when he wrote about what conversion of heart means. One of his stages of conversion is the way we approach our ordinary life. It speaks to us about our basic perspective of our own daily life. Fr. Lonergan says that conversion of heart is a change from viewing life as a series of problems, just one darn thing after another, to seeing life as a mystery, a wonder, a surprise, a gift of God.

Let's try that when we wake up tomorrow morning and look at ourselves in the mirror. I have to say that more often than not, my early morning review of the day looks more like one darn thing after another than a wonderful, surprising gift.

A friend gave me a coffee mug. Usually coffee mugs have words and designs on the outside. This one had a message inside so it was right before my eyes every time I took a sip. What was the message? It said, "Life is a gift." I wonder why he gave that to me. Probably because I need this homily more than you do.

I am not being a Pollyanna about all this. I know and you know that our lives are filled with routines, tasks, and obligations. That will not change. But we can change. We can wake up to the coming of the Lord in the world around us and the world within us.

How many times each day does Jesus come to us in the world around us? He comes in the people we meet, and in the ordinary circumstances of the day. Yes, even in our routines, if we will only wake up and see him. How many times each day does Jesus come to us in the world within us? He comes in those little inner promptings. He comes in those unexpected moments of clarity and sensed presence, if only we will wake up to his constant comings in our hearts. How will the coming of Jesus at Christmas really mean anything to us if we are not awake to all the ways he comes to us each day in and around us?

That's our simple and childlike approach to Advent. We want to be more like three-year-old Alexia. Let's remember each morning when we look at ourselves in the mirror to pray simply, "Lord, wake me up to this new day." If we do, Advent will be full of surprise and wonder.

📖 Second Sunday of Advent
(Is 11:1-10; Rom 15:4-9; Mt 3:1-12)

In today's Gospel we see the great figure of John the Baptist. And what is John's message today? "Repent, for the kingdom of heaven is at hand." Shortly, we will see what this means, but first, let's see what it does not mean.

Picture a TV evangelist at a revival meeting. He has been preaching about repentance, and then he has an altar call. "All of you, who repent, come forward. All of you, who accept Jesus as your savior, come to the altar." When everyone gathers there he proclaims over them that they are saved. I'm not saying this is bad, but it is not enough. And this is not what John the Baptist meant when he called people to repent.

Let's translate John's message to our situation today. If John the Baptist was preaching here today he would say to you and to me, "Repent, for the kingdom of heaven is at hand. Don't pride yourselves for being Catholics. I tell you God can make Catholics out of these desert stones." John is saying, "Don't think you have it made because Abraham is your father. Don't think you are saved because you are Israelites, members of God's chosen people." John shatters the security that comes from being part of any group. John is saying, "God wants more from you than professing the true religion. God wants you to repent."

So we've got his message. Can we say, "Thank you, John"? Or do we feel like saying, "My God, John, what are you asking of us?" John asks of us exactly the same that Jesus asks of us. Jesus began his public ministry with the same call, "The kingdom of heaven is at hand. Reform your lives." What do Jesus and John mean? What does it mean to repent and reform?

It is much more than responding to an altar call. It is more than repenting of our sins. It is deeper than anything we do. It means changing who we are. As Paul described it, it is putting on a new person, taking on the values, attitudes, and priorities of Jesus. It is like reaching down inside and turning our self inside out from the toes up. It is becoming a new person. It will not happen with one decision or one moment of change. It is a process that will go on for as long as we live.

Now the big question: How can we do this? And the big answer is: We can't do this. We can't reach down inside and turn our self inside out. We can't make our self into a new person. We don't even know what our new self would look like. But God can do it. God wants to do it. God will do it, if we want him to. That's the big "if." We might believe, "Hey,

I'm not a bad person. Let's leave well enough alone because, honestly, becoming a new person sounds kind of scary."

Let us ask God to reform us and we will see just how wonderful and surprising Advent will be. God is waiting for us to say yes. God waited once before for a big yes which changed the world and resulted in Christmas. God waited for a young maiden named Mary to say, "Yes, Lord, let it be done to me as you will." Now it's our turn. Can we say the same, "Yes, Lord, let it be done to me as you will"? If we can, each new day will be a wonder and a surprise, just as wonderful and surprising as our God.

Third Sunday of Advent
(Is 35:1-6, 10; Jas 5:7-10; Mt 11:2-11)

Jesus said, "Blessed is the one who takes no offense at me." To take offense at someone means that we find fault with that person. It means that person has hurt or disappointed us in some way. It may be that we are uncomfortable around that person, and certainly we would not choose to be close to someone at whom we take offense.

Is there anyone among us who feels this way about Jesus? We probably answer, "Of course not. We love Jesus and want to be close to him. Certainly we don't take offense at Jesus." But we need to reflect on this a bit more. Why did the Jewish religious leaders take offense at Jesus? Why did so many people find fault with Jesus that he ended up nailed to a cross? The answer to that is that Jesus asked too much. He asked for more than many people were willing to give.

We will not take offense at Jesus as long as we don't take him too seriously. We won't take offense at Jesus as long as we settle for being comfortable Christians. A comfortable Christian is one who goes to Mass, prays daily and tries to do what is right, but who finds no challenge from Jesus beyond that. Isn't that the story of the Pharisees? They worshipped and prayed faithfully and they observed all their holy days. But they certainly took offense at Jesus because they knew he was asking for more. Is it possible that we can take offense at Jesus? Yes, we can if we take him seriously and if we reflect on what he is really asking of us.

When we reflect it becomes clear that Jesus asks everything of us. He asks for complete trust in him. He asks for our whole hearts and selves. He asks for everything we have. He asks us to place all we are and all we have into his hands and trust that he wants only the best for us.

When we realize what is dearest to us and what we cling to, we realize what it is Jesus is asking of us. What is dearest to us? Is it our life and our health? Is it our loved ones? Is it our good reputation and the regards people have for us? Is it our money and our security? It is anything we hold to for dear life. All of this is what Jesus wants us to place in his hands with trust.

Why do we refuse to let go? Why do we hesitate? It is because we still do not trust Jesus. We are afraid that when Jesus asks for all we are and all we have, he will take it from us. We fear that if we place it all in his hands, we are placing it in jeopardy. If we offer our health, we'll probably get sick. If we offer our reputation, we will probably be slandered. If we offer our money, we'll probably end up poor. We fear that when we get too close to Jesus we will suffer for it. These fears can be very real, but when we think about it, isn't it ridiculous?

Right now God can do anything he wants with us and with what we have. It's already all in God's hands but God wants us to turn it over to him with trusting hearts. God wants us to believe in his love and care. God does not want our health, our money, or our reputation. God just wants our heart. God needs us to freely give our heart. He will not force that gift. It needs to be freely given.

📖 Fourth Sunday of Advent
(Is 7:10-14; Rom 1:1-7; Mt 1:18-24)

Last week we talked about Jesus wanting us to trust him completely. Today I want to look deeper into the trust that he asks of us. The Gospel is all about trust, but we need to understand this Gospel if we want the full impact of the trust involved in it.

Did you notice in the Gospel that Mary is betrothed to Joseph, yet Mary is called Joseph's wife? Maybe you're wondering, "Were they engaged or married? We need to understand what Jewish betrothal and marriage were 2,000 years ago. Betrothal was the first part of marriage and actually made a man and woman husband and wife. But they did not live together. Some months after betrothal the husband took his wife into his home at which time normal married life began.

Today's Gospel is situated between Joseph's and Mary's betrothal and their living together. We are told that Mary was with child. Can we imagine how Joseph felt about this? Can we imagine his anger, frustration, and disappointment over this? But Joseph was a good man and decided to divorce

Mary quietly to protect her reputation. Then Joseph had a dream. He was told in his dream not to be afraid to take Mary into his home, for it was through the Holy Spirit that this child had been conceived.

Did you ever wake up from a dream and wonder what that was all about? Joseph trusted his dream and trusted the child was from the Holy Spirit, whatever that meant. So our first lesson in trust is this good man Joseph.

Prior to Father's Day a retreat master was speaking to a group of dads. He said to them, "Joseph is the perfect model of trust in God for you men." One of the dads immediately challenged him, "Wait a minute! What do you mean? Joseph's situation was totally different from mine. Joseph was a saint. His wife was sinless and his child was the Son of God." The retreat master stuck to his guns. He responded, "Was your wife pregnant before your marriage and you didn't know by whom? Were you ordered to make a long trip by donkey days before your wife was to deliver your child? And when you got there, you found no place to stay. Doesn't a woman deserve some privacy and comfort to give birth? Was your baby born in a cave and placed in a feeding trough for his crib? Don't you think Joseph wondered, 'Are you sure you know what you're doing, Lord? Are you really looking after us, Lord?'" Without doubt, Joseph is our first lesson in trust.

Sometimes our trust is shaken when we are suffering and struggling with something. Like Joseph, we wonder, "God, if you love me so much, why don't you help me? God, I would not treat someone I love this way. God, are you sure you know what you're doing?"

I learn another lesson in trust every time I visit with the homeless in our winter shelter. At one dinner the woman to my right was pregnant with twins. She was happy about that and she didn't even have a home. How could they survive? Would I have that much trust? The woman sitting across the table from me had a story that would make your hair stand up. For years she struggled with alcohol addiction. She had lost two daughters to foster care. Yes, she said she was mad at God for quite a while, but now she had Jesus back in her heart. She believed she would recover and find a house and get her family back. Could I trust that much?

Joseph's whole life was filled with things that did not seem to make sense and with things that made him wonder and doubt. Sometimes our lives are filled the same way. It is especially during times like these that Jesus asks us to trust in this way.

📖 CHRISTMAS
(Is 9:1-6; Ti 2:11-14; Lk 2:1-14)

We often hear that Christmas is a bigger day for children than for adults. Why is that? It is because children are full of wonder. Their eyes get as big as saucers. Their faces light up in amazement. They are full of questions. When we grow up we seem to lose some of that. We become sophisticated and forget to wonder. We are more interested in finding answers to questions than wondering about them. What a shame. No wonder Jesus said that we must become like little children to enter the kingdom of heaven.

So, will you wonder with me? Can we be kids again? Can our eyes still get as big as saucers? Let's do it.

About the year 85 A.D., a genius named Luke wrote a Gospel. We just heard a little of it. In one line Luke opens the door to wonder and gives us a glimpse of the mystery and wonder that we celebrate today. In one line Luke tells us what really happened at Christmas. Listen carefully.

"She gave birth to her son – the firstborn – and wrapped him in swaddling clothes." Let's unpack that one line to come to the real mystery of Christmas. The title "firstborn" is used only a few times in the New Testament. Listen. "Jesus Christ is the firstborn from the dead and ruler of the kings of the earth." "God leads his firstborn into the world – let all the angels worship him." "He is the firstborn of all creation."

Mary gave birth to the firstborn – to the almighty God of all creation – then she wrapped him in swaddling clothes. What are swaddling clothes? They were long bands of cloth. It was customary to wrap newborn babies tightly in swaddling clothes so they would feel secure. If their arms and legs were left loose to flop around, the baby would feel threatened by this strange, new world.

Do we hear what Luke is telling us? Mary gave birth to the firstborn of all creation and wrapped him in swaddling clothes so the creator of the universe would not feel threatened by the world he created.

What is the wonder and mystery that we celebrate today? It is that God himself became a human being like us. We cannot fathom this. Our eyes should be getting bigger. All we can do is wonder in our amazement. Why in the world would God want to become one of us? There is only one reason. "God so loved the world he sent his only son" (Jn 3). God loves you and me so much that he had to come to save us. Today a savior is born.

Can this really be true? Can God love me that much? The great theologian, St. Thomas Aquinas, wrote, "If you were the only person in human history who needed to be saved, the universe would have stood in awe as God came to earth just for you."

Words fail us. It is all too much. It is love beyond our imagination. It is love we need to remember the next time we are feeling down, feeling unloved or unappreciated. But, my friends, it is true. Christmas really did happen. Christmas is real.

I close with one of my favorite quotes from Bishop Fulton J. Sheen about Christmas, "These human hearts of ours can be cold enough, God knows. Still, the human heart must have a melting point. The melting point must be the cave – and – God crying – a baby."

📖 Holy Family
(Sir 3:2-7, 12-14; Col 3:12-21; Mt 2:13-15, 19-23)

Today is the Feast of the Holy Family and today we honor Jesus, Mary, and Joseph. Today we also honor your family.

We celebrate fathers who would do anything for their families. They work hard to support their families. They love them so much they would die for them. Yes, ordinary fathers, when we think about them, can be and are real heroes, just like Joseph, your model.

We celebrate mothers who love as only mothers can love. Isn't it true that mothers can never stop being mothers? They will worry and pray for their children as long as they live. I visited my mother in her nursing home apartment when she was about 90 years old. A friend dropped in while I was there and asked Mom how her five kids were doing. Her five kids were all in their 60's, but Mom answered, "I think they are all doing well – so far." Mothers, keep loving and praying, just like Mary, your model.

We celebrate your own flesh and blood, your children. It takes a good part of your life and energy to raise a child. And it is true; children do not always seem to appreciate it. But they grow up and grow in their love and appreciation. We celebrate all those children who do obey and help to make home the loving place it is, and all those teenagers who really try to live right with all the pressure around them to do otherwise. You are just like Jesus, your model.

So today we celebrate all of you and thank God for you. You might say, "But we do have our problems." Of course you do. That is part of normal family life. There is an old song that says, "You always hurt the one you love, the one you shouldn't hurt at all." That's strange but true, isn't it? Why is this true? It is true because our loved ones are closest to us and always with us and around us. We are different people and different people can rub against each other, get in each other's way, and see things in different ways. Consequently, loved ones have more opportunity to hurt and be hurt. It is true because we love our family so much we invest much of ourselves in them. When we love, we are more vulnerable to being hurt. It hurts more when our values conflict. We are more prone to be disappointed with one another.

But please remember, all of this is part of normal family life. No wonder Paul says in our second reading after he gave the qualities of healthy family life: kindness, humility, meekness, and patience, that forgiveness is all important. We need to forgive whatever grievances we have against one another. We need to forgive as the Lord has forgiven us. So, as true as the song is, "We always hurt the one who love," we need to add another line, "We always forgive the ones we love."

We have much to celebrate today – all of you. And now we ask God's blessing on all of you.

📖 Epiphany
(Is 60:1-6; Eph 3:2-3a, 5-6; Mt 2:1-12)

Epiphany means a manifestation, a showing forth. In our Gospel, it was the Epiphany star that manifested to the three kings the arrival of Jesus. Jesus' message is called the epiphany of God the Father. Jesus grew up to show us who our God really is. He manifested a God who loves us totally and unconditionally; a God who cares so much about each one of us that he knows the number of hairs on our heads; a God who is rich in mercy and forgives our sins with great joy in heaven. Jesus was such a perfect epiphany of God that when Phillip asked him, "Show us the Father and that will be enough for us," Jesus replied, "Phillip, he who sees me sees the Father."

Jesus manifested a God so loving and appealing, that he is hard to resist. The world of Jesus needed to hear that because they had not known God that way. Their God was a distant power they held in great awe, but could not personally relate to. What an eye-opening manifestation of God Jesus was to them.

Does our world today need the same epiphany? Do we

desperately need to know this loving and appealing God? Yes, perhaps now more than ever. Why do people today say they want to be more spiritual, but at the same time say they are disaffected with organized religion? We hear this all the time, don't we? Some people say, "I pray and I want to be more spiritual, but I don't need the church."

For the answer to that we need to look at ourselves. Why? You and I are the epiphany of God in our world today. That's right. Whether we like it or not, we are. We are the people who publicly profess our faith in Jesus. We are people who believe Jesus died for us to save us from our sins. We are the people who believe Jesus rose from the dead and showed us our own future resurrection to new life. Who else will people look to?

What kind of epiphany are we? When nonbelievers look at us, when people who are searching for God look to us, what do they see? Are we fearful believers? Fearful people have grim looks. They are so serious because religion for them is serious business. They fear for their salvation. Do grim, serious, fearful people manifest a loving and appealing God?

Are we a legal epiphany? Is our faith a collection of rule books? Over Christmas I heard a person criticize her pastor for not announcing that New Year's Day was not a holyday of obligation. She said people needed to know because if they thought it was a holyday and did not go to mass, they would be guilty of sin. I heard another person complain about a priest who made it all sound too easy. Apparently, he had said that "We are all good people. God loves us no matter what we have done. God has forgiven us. So rejoice." I asked her, "Well, isn't that all true?" "Well," she said, "maybe it is, but it's all too easy. We should make it more difficult."

Does our faith with all its laws lay heavy on us? Do people who are burdened with their religion manifest a loving and appealing God? Are we an epiphany of the God Jesus showed us? When people observe us do they see people who smile a lot because there's so much to smile about, who can find hope and meaning even in life's most difficult circumstances, who love and care for other people because they know how much they are loved, who are tolerant and forgiving because they know how much they have been forgiven? Are we a manifestation of this loving and appealing God?

We are. I see it every time I celebrate liturgy with you, every time I sense the joy and love when we come together, every time a newcomer says to me, "This is such a friendly parish, I want to be a part of it." I see it every time a suffering person smiles and thanks God for his goodness, when our homeless guests are welcomed and respected as God's people, and when a St. Vincent de Paul volunteer says he feels blessed every time he visits the poor.

There is no Epiphany star in the heavens today. It is us. We are called to be the lights leading to a God who is irresistible. Keep shining.

📖 Baptism of Jesus
(Is 42:1-4, 6-7; Acts 10:34-38; Mt 3:13-17)

In today's Gospel Jesus was baptized by John in the Jordan River. John's baptism was one of repentance, of turning away from sin. Jesus did not need to repent because he was sinless, but he was baptized anyway because baptism means more than forgiveness of sin. Jesus' baptism was his decision to live the will of his Father – come what may. Jesus went into the desert for forty days of self examination and confronting temptation. He wrestled with the demons who tempted him to be someone other than his Father called him to be. He was faithful to his Father and overcame his temptations. Jesus remained faithful to the end when he prayed in the garden, "Not my will but yours, Father, be done," and then left the garden to suffer and die.

Our Church teaches us that our baptism also forgives sin. If we were baptized as infants that probably did not mean too much for us, but when adults are baptized all is completely forgiven up to that moment. They start again as new people. Our Church also teaches us that our baptism is more than forgiveness of sin. It is so much more. It was one of, if not the, most important days of our life. We need to reflect on this because most of us probably don't think about it very often. We just take it for granted.

It is sad to say, but some people baptize their babies just because that's the thing to do. It means no more than that to them. It reminds me of the story of three priests who got together for coffee. They discovered that all their churches had problems with bats infesting their bell towers. The bats were really making a mess. "I got so mad," one priest said, "I took a shotgun and fired at them. It made holes in the ceiling but did not hurt the bats." The second priest said, "I tried trapping them alive. Then I drove fifty miles before releasing them but they beat me back to the church." The third priest said, "I haven't had any more problems." "What did you do?" the others asked. "I simply baptized them and I haven't seen them since."

If I ask you, "Are you baptized?" you probably would say, "Of course I'm baptized. I've got a certificate to prove it." But if I ask you, "What is the date of your baptism?" Could you tell me? You would probably say, "Let me look at my certificate." But when we reflect on the importance of that day, we should be celebrating it at least as much as we celebrate our birthday.

To be honest with you, I had to check my certificate. Now I know my important day, September 12th. I noted it on my calendar because I intend to celebrate September 12 from now on. Why should we celebrate? Because when we were baptized in the name of the Father, the Son, and the Holy Spirit, we were dedicated to God in a very special way. We were not just children anymore. We became children of God.

As Jesus began his public life of faithfulness to his Father with his baptism, you and I were put on the same road. With the help of our parents and many others we were brought up to know Jesus and his teachings, to show the Father's love and care for us, to be strengthened with the sacraments to wrestle with our own demons, and to live the Father's will to the end, come what may.

What a momentous day our baptism was. We should celebrate it. How do we do that? We celebrate it by thanking God for wanting us to be his family. We celebrate by thanking God for making us his children and, along with Jesus, the heirs to the kingdom of heaven. We celebrate by renewing our resolution to live our baptism faithfully, come what may.

In our Gospels, when Jesus came up from the waters of the Jordan River, the heavens opened and a voice said, "This is my Beloved Son with whom I am well pleased." At our baptism that same voice said to you and to me, "This is my beloved child with whom I am well pleased. Go now and live your baptism." Isn't that something to celebrate?

📖 Second Sunday of the Year
(Is 49:3, 5-6; 1 Cor 1:1-3; Jn 1:29-34)

We are all theologians. Oh, we may not be professional theologians with degrees from theological institutions, but nevertheless, we are theologians. The word "theology" comes from two Greek words. "Theos," which means God, and "logia," which means study, combine to make theology, the study of God.

We have been learning about God all our lives from our parents, teachers, priests, and friends. Each of us has a theology of God. If I were to ask you who your God was, you would give me a description of what your God is like. That is your theology of God.

Our theology of God is not just theoretical. It is operative, meaning it affects every aspect of our lives. Our theology of God determines how we pray, what we think of ourselves, and how we relate to others and the world around us. It determines our whole outlook on life. It shapes our hopes, fears, and dreams. Our theology of God is the most operative thing in our lives. Everything else depends on it.

What is your theology of God? How do you see God? How do we know our theology is correct or needs adjustment? The norm we have is scripture, God's word. All theology must be tested constantly against the truth of God's word.

God's word today gives us another chance to test our theology. Test yours as I test mine with today's Gospel. John the Baptist saw Jesus coming toward him and said…said what? Did he say, "Oh my God, he's here and he knows your every thought, word, and deed"? Did he say, "Behold, here comes the judge. Your life better add up right"? Or did he say, "Behold, the Lamb of God, who will pull you up straight, will punish you, will make you pay for your sins"?

Does this fit your theology of God? If it does, you should feel pretty tense when you think of God. You should feel afraid and cautious. You are walking on eggshells around God. If it does fit, then we have an even bigger problem because our theology of God is simply wrong. The most operative thing in our life is off base. What affects every aspect of our life is false and this fouls up everything about us.

What did John the Baptist say when he saw Jesus? He said, "Behold, the Lamb of God who takes away the sins of the world." The sin of the world is your sin and my sin. The Lamb of God takes away our sin and when God takes it away, it is gone. In God's mind, it is like it never happened. That's the truth of God's word. That is correct theology.

Does this fit our theology of God? Is our God one who comes to save, not condemn? Does our God forgive and not punish? Do we believe in a God who loves us no matter what we have done? Is this theology operative in our lives?

If it is, we can value ourselves as loved people, we can love God and others because we are loved, we can get on with our life, leaving behind past mistakes and sins, and we can simply relax and enjoy God.

Theology is not some esoteric, abstract subject for monks and mystics to ponder. It is the most practical and operative force in our lives. Our personal theology makes a difference. It's time to check it out.

📖 Third Sunday of the Year
(Is 8:23-9:3; 1 Cor 1:10-13, 17; Mt 4:12-23)

In today's Gospel Jesus begins his public life. He preaches, "Repent, for the kingdom of heaven is at hand." This is the theme song of his whole ministry. If we miss the theme, we miss the whole thing.

What does Jesus mean when Jesus says to us, "Repent"? He means much more than repenting of our sins. The Greek word is "Metanoia," which means a basic change of heart or mind. Jesus means repent of who we are, not just what we do. Paul writes that it is becoming a new person.

This may be much more than we are used to thinking. It's a lot easier to settle for less. For example, if our Christian life is just a list of teachings, we are missing the deeper reality. Teachings we have, but repenting of who we are is much more than any formula of faith. Remember, the apostles were long gone before the Apostles' Creed was formulated. Is the extent of our Christian life following a set of rules and laws? Rules and laws we must have, but repenting of who we are is much more than any code of conduct.

To repent of whom we are, to become a new person, means making the values and goals of Jesus our own. It means seeing as God sees and judging as God judges. We are not talking about cosmetic change. Jesus calls us to an extreme makeover. The psychologist, Abraham Maslow, had an interesting response to the question of why so few people leave all to follow a dream or to pursue a noble goal. He said, "We are afraid to become what we are capable of being. We thrill at the possibility, but we also shudder at it."

Look at it this way. Every mom and dad want their children to be the very best they can be. What parent would say to a child, "You don't have to try too hard. We'll settle for mediocre. Second-rate is good enough for us." When Jesus asks us to repent of who we are, he is simply calling us to be the best we can be. Part of us is thrilled at the possibility, but another part shudders because it sounds too scary.

Are we afraid to become what we are capable of being because we might have to change too much or because we might become too different? Do we really want to be different people or would we prefer to stay as we are because we are more comfortable and secure with ourselves as we are now? Someone wrote, "I can think of only one person who welcomes change, a wet baby."

When Jesus calls us to repent, he is just asking us to open up and let God do it. God has passionate love for us. He will not hurt us. God's passionate love for us can work miracles in us. His love can remake us into the complete and beautiful people he knows we can be.

You are probably familiar with the musical, "Man of La Mancha." It is the story of Don Quixote, who is ridiculed because he lives the illusion of being a knight of old. He is laughed at because he battles windmills that he imagines are dragons. Near the end, Don Quixote is dying and at his side is Aldonza, a scorned prostitute whom he had idolized. He called her Dulcinea, sweet one. Others had laughed and ridiculed his vision of her, but Don Quixote had loved her in a way unlike anything she had ever experienced. When Don Quixote breathed his last, Aldonza begins to sing "The Impossible Dream." As the song dies away, someone shouts to her, "Aldonza." She pulls herself up proudly and responds, "My name is Dulcinea." The crazy knight's love had transformed her. Just as God's crazy love for us will make us the new people that Jesus calls us to be.

Fourth Sunday of the Year
(Zep 2:3; 3:12-13; 1Cor 1:26-31; Mt 5:1-12a)

Beatitude is blissful happiness. Today's Gospel, which is the first of nine beatitudes, is perhaps the most misunderstood line in the Gospels. "Blessed are the poor in spirit, for theirs is the kingdom of heaven." We all want to be "poor in spirit" don't we, because the kingdom of heaven is theirs? But what does "poor in spirit" mean?

Being poor in spirit has nothing to do with bank balances. Jesus does not want us all to be poor. In fact, Jesus calls us to help raise people out of poverty. Being poor in spirit does not refer to people with money who are spiritually detached from their money, or who are not consumed and driven by money concerns, or who have not made money a god in their lives.

To get closer to the true meaning of poor in spirit let's look at some differences that come to mind when we contrast rich and poor. I am not saying that these words apply to every rich or poor person. They are simply words that come to mind when we think of rich and poor in general terms.

Rich speaks of self-sufficiency, independence, power and control, of a certain arrogance and assertiveness over others. In short, the rich are the "haves." Poor speaks of neediness, of dependence, of powerlessness, of lowly and humble posture. The poor are the "have-nots."

Now we are getting closer to the real meaning of poor in spirit. We find the truth in the original Hebrew word for poor in spirit, "the Anawim." Our first two readings speak of the Anawim. Zephaniah says, "I will leave in your midst a people humble and lowly who shall take refuge in the Lord." Paul says, "God chose the lowly who count for nothing to reduce to nothing those who are something, so that no human being might boast before God."

People are the Anawim, the poor in spirit, because of how they relate to God. That's the key. How do we see ourselves in relationship to God? How do we stand before God? Are we the haves or have-nots? Are we self-sufficient, doing quite nicely on our own or do we have a desperate need of God? Do we feel powerful and in control or do we feel our powerlessness? Do we feel spiritually rich, full of good deeds and merits or do we feel spiritually poor?

Lord, have mercy on me, a sinner. Lord, without you I can do nothing.

It's all about how we stand before God. Being poor in spirit is simply living the truth. What have we that cannot be taken from us this very day: our money, success, reputation, health, life itself? What are we that cannot vanish this very day: our virtues, talents, personal strengths?

The truth is that everything we have and are is completely dependent on God. The kingdom of heaven is ours, not because we deserve it, but because Jesus died on the cross to give us heaven. Paul wrote, "If we think we are justified by our good works, then Jesus died in vain." If we are feeling a desperate need of God, we are the blessed Anawim.

When our final moment of truth finds us standing before God will we want to trust in ourselves, our accomplishments, or anything about ourselves? Or will we want to trust in God's love for us, a love that brings us to beatitude, that blissful state of happiness? I know what I want to trust in. How about you?

Fifth Sunday of the Year
(Is 58:7-10; 1 Cor 2:1-5; Mt 5:13-16)

Most of us are more conscious of our weaknesses than our strengths and of our sins than our virtues. That's why most of us find it difficult to accept compliments graciously. If someone said to you, "You are a good person. You inspire me." how would you react? You would probably feel embarrassed and say something like, "Oh, not really. If you knew me better you would not say that."

Now listen to Jesus in today's Gospel. He says to you and me, "You are the salt of the earth; you are the light of the world." How do we react to that? Do we say, "Oh, Lord, if you knew me better you would not say that"? Do we say, "Not me, Lord, You can find someone a lot better than me to call salt and light"?

Why do we hesitate to apply Jesus' words to ourselves? It is because we sense the powerful meaning of the images he uses. Salt gives flavor and zest to food. Jesus said we are the salt of the earth. We give flavor to life, zest to living, and courage, hope, and joy to a world which is flat and tired.

Light is equally powerful. We do not appreciate light until we experience darkness. Jesus said we are the light of the world, a world which suffers from all shades of darkness, a world groping about looking for some light, meaning, and sense to it all. Can Jesus be serious? Does he really mean this? Yes, Jesus is serious. We are the ones who do not take this seriously because we do not see in ourselves the truth of what Jesus says about us.

What a shame because when I look out at you I see a church filled with salt and light. We are surrounded by salt and light. We are constantly inspired by people we get to know. I am inspired by people in the confessional and in my office who share with me their successes and failures, hopes and dreams. I see such goodness in you. How often I say to myself, "Thank you, Lord, for this person." I have seen more salt and light.

I am inspired by the sick, like the woman who had been bedridden with arthritis for years. Every time I visited her in the nursing home she had a smile and was full of love for everyone. One day she was having a really bad day and complained about the noise others in her room were making. Then immediately she asked my pardon because she had no reason to complain. God is so good. Every time I saw her I left a better person for being in her presence. Dear woman, you have no idea what salt and light you are.

We see it all around us. We see it in the mother who keeps washing, cooking, loving, and giving her best, even though sometimes she feels like trading in her life for a different one. We see it in the father who keeps working long hours, perhaps at something he does not enjoy, because he will do anything for his family he loves so much. We see it in the young person who says no to sex and drugs because no is more than a refusal, it is a yes to Jesus and his values.

Oh yes, Jesus was serious. We are surrounded by salt and light. You and I are salt and light to each other and to everyone we touch when we live gospel values.

Get in touch with your power for goodness and let's go forth to add a dash of salt and turn on a few more lights.

📖 First Sunday of Lent
(Gn 2:7-9, 3:17; Rom 5:12-19; Mt 4:1-11)

Our Church tells us we are a pilgrim people, that is, a people on the way, on a journey together, and a people who have not yet arrived. The journey we are on is not a trip to the coast or even a trip around the world. Our journey is our life, which leads to death, which leads to resurrection.

Sometimes I forget that this life is not a dress rehearsal. I sometimes think that I don't have to take it too seriously, that I am just practicing for the real life that comes later. But *this* trip is it.

Thank God that we are again in Lent, that blessed season of the year when we are called to look at ourselves and our lives. This self examination will prevent us from just tip toeing through life and waking up some day asking, "Who am I? What have I been all about? Have I missed the boat?" Lent calls us to deal with these questions now so they will not take us by surprise later.

We have Jesus as our model in today's gospel. We see Jesus struggling with the same questions with which we struggle.

The temptations which Jesus faced in the desert are more profound that they may appear to be. Jesus had a growing sense of his mission and purpose in life, and he had a growing awareness of the suffering involved in fulfilling that mission.

Jesus knew what the people expected. They wanted a powerful messiah, a king, a person who would lift their nation to great power and prosperity. He knew how tough it can be when one chooses not to meet the expectations of others.

The temptations of Jesus touched the very core of who he was and what he was all about. "Show your power," he heard them say. "Be our leader. We will applaud you, reward you, and offer you great success and influence. We want you at the top. Be our king!" But Jesus overcame his profound temptation. He chose not to meet the expectations of others, but to be faithful to his own mission. Jesus came out of the desert inviting us to do the same; "Reform your lives and believe the Good News," he proclaimed. The word "reform" is too weak. To understand what Jesus is calling us to we need to go back to the original Greek word, "metanoia." Metanoia means a basic change of heart, a change of attitude. It means a re-evaluation of our goals and values, and of our basic stance in life. It is a reformation not of what we do, but of who we are.

Jesus calls us to look into the center of our hearts, into our very core where we find our values. We call them values because they are so valuable, so dear to us. We don't want to let go of them. Our values are the driving force in our lives. They make us act and react the way we do. Our values tell us what we are all about and what we want from life.

How do we get to our core? How do we know what our values are? I believe questions like these are helpful: What do I really want from life? Where are my main interests? What excites me and animates me? What do I like to talk about? What do I daydream about? How do I spend most of my energy? Who do I want to become? How do I want to be remembered? It is a challenge to do this. We may hesitate because we are afraid of what we may find.

Throughout our lives we are tempted to be someone else, to be someone less than we really are. In our youth we are tempted to forget who we are in order to be accepted by the crowd, to be liked, accepted and popular. As adults we are tempted to take on the values of the world around us, including values that promise profit and prestige and the rewards that come to those who play the game.

Jesus took that deep look within himself. He struggled with the temptation to be someone other than who he was called to be. Now he calls us to take the same look during these

Lenten days. I don't know about you, but I need to take another look.

I hope we will have a Lenten season like Jesus' forty days in the desert. I hope we will take the time to reflect on who we are. We are more than 100 pounds of clay. We are more than plumbers, housewives, lawyers, and nurses. We are more than what we do. We are God's children. We are dedicated by baptism to live as disciples of Jesus. We are loved by God. We are saved by Jesus. We are called to live the values of Jesus, and we are destined to live forever with the God who loves and saves us.

Lent is a blessed, precious time. Let us use it to rediscover our true selves and to settle for nothing less.

📖 Second Sunday of Lent
(Gn 12:1-4a; 2 Tim 1:8b-10; Mt 17:1-9)

Does life sort of catch up with you sometimes? Does it get burdensome and scary? Do you feel very alone with your problems and your fears? Do you sometimes feel like circling the wagons and hanging on for dear life? When we feel this way, we really need what God offers us in today's readings. They speak to us about the faith that gives us courage, and about the trust that carries us into the unknown with confidence.

Think of your best friend. When we really believe and trust in someone, we feel comfortable and secure with that person. We know we can depend on that person no matter what happens. We feel deep loneliness when we don't have that kind of dependable friend.

What about with God? Do we feel comfortable and secure with God? Do we know we can depend on Jesus no matter what happens? When life gets rough, do we think of Jesus as our dependable friend or do we just tough it out alone?

In today's readings about transfiguration it is evident that

Peter, James, and John had some kind of mystical experience of the divinity of Jesus. For a moment they saw that Jesus was more than he appeared to be. Jesus was someone in whom they could believe and whom they could trust. Peter, James, and John would need that faith and trust very soon. Jesus was about to enter into his suffering and death. This would be devastating to his disciples. From all appearances, Jesus was going to fail miserably and die like a common criminal. The disciples' whole world would be shaken, and their expectations would be dashed to nothingness. After an adventure with Jesus that had seemed so full of promise, it would be back to the fishing boats. So, in today's readings Jesus shows his disciples for a brief moment that no matter what happens, they can believe in him and trust him.

As we consider faith and trust, we can look at Abraham in our first reading. He was 75 years old, enjoying the comfort of retirement, and looking forward to his last years in peace and security. Then God called him to give it all up. "Go forth from the land of your kinsfolk to a strange land I will show you. I will make of you a great nation." In absolute faith and trust, Abraham uprooted himself, left his family and friends, and moved to a strange, new place. Abraham risked everything on the promise that God would make of him a great nation. Remember, at 75 years of age Abraham and his wife were childless. So it took great faith.

When we have a little of Abraham's faith and trust, it takes a load off our shoulders. God wants us to be responsible people, but all the responsibility is not ours. Sometimes we take ourselves so seriously that we are like the bird in the Buddhist story. This bird was lying on its back with its legs raised rigidly against the sky. Other birds thought the behavior peculiar and asked him what he was doing. "Why don't you straighten out and fly right," they asked. "I'll tell you why," the strange bird responded, "I am holding up the sky." Don't we get that way at times? Sometimes I feel so burdened with things not going well with the Church and I have to stop and pray, "Hey Lord, it's your Church, not mine. You are the savior of the world, not me."

We are basically insecure people. We constantly look for assurances and guarantees. We limit ourselves terribly because of our fears. As we grow in faith and trust, our lives open up and we become bigger people. Faith raises us above our need for absolute security and allows us to take a healthy risk. If we need absolute assurance that we will not drown, we will never push off from the side of the pool the first time. If Abraham had not risked everything there would not have been a chosen people or a promised land.

Jesus wants to transfigure our lives with faith and trust. He wants to lighten our load and open up our possibilities in life. Which way will we have it? We can bear our burden alone or we can remember we are not alone. We can lie on our back, holding up the sky or we can straighten up and fly.

📖 Third Sunday of Lent
(Ex 17:3-7; Rom 5:1-2, 5-8; Jn 4:5-42)

The mysterious conversation between Jesus and the Samaritan woman brings us in touch with the mystery of our religious life. It shows us that everything we do in our religious life we base on faith and that without faith it makes no sense.

What is this nebulous thing we call faith? The dictionary defines faith as the "firm belief in something for which there is no proof." Does this make sense? It does to believers. Believers are able to put their faith in something beyond their grasp, beyond their understanding. Faith is such a powerful force. It is truly remarkable.

Our faith urges us to live our lives "as best we can" according to the Gospel values of Jesus. "As best we can" is an important phrase because none of us live those values perfectly. We all fail and have to start again. We do the best we can and even God cannot ask more of us than that. What does Jesus promise us for living our lives as best we can? He promises eternal life. This promise immediately calls us to even more faith.

We do not understand eternal life. We know nothing about it. Jesus promised eternal life to those who care about others. "Come blessed of my Father, inherit the kingdom prepared for you from the foundation of the world…for I was hungry and you gave me to eat." The "Me Generation" says "I am all that counts. I need to take care of myself. I need to fulfill all my wishes and desires. I only go through life once so I need to grab all I can for myself." Why should we care about others? Because we believe that God wants us to care. But without faith, unselfish care of others does not make much sense.

Jesus said, "I am the living bread. If anyone eats this bread, he will live forever." How often do we hear others say they don't want to go to Mass because they get nothing out of it? They say that Mass is boring and homilies are dull. It really does not make much sense without faith. If we do not believe that something very important happens underneath our imperfect ways of celebrating liturgy, we might as well stay home. But Jesus said, "I am the living bread. If anyone eats this bread he will live forever." We can't see it, we can't prove it. We either believe or we don't.

In today's readings Jesus says, "The water I give shall become a fountain leaping up to provide eternal life." He uses the metaphor of living water to tell us that our faith and trust in him produces something important. He tells us that a loving relationship with him is alive and makes a big difference. He says that when we believe and live according to his values, his presence in us becomes a fountain leaping up to eternal life.

I can't prove any of this to you. You can't prove any of this to anyone. We either believe it or we don't. Why are you here now? It must be because you believe. Why do you believe? Because God has gifted you with faith and you have accepted his gift.

Our day-to-day life can be mysterious enough. Sometimes we search desperately for meaning, sense, and purpose in what we do and in what happens to us. Sometimes we wonder what it all adds up to. Jesus tells us it all adds up to an even bigger mystery – eternal life.

Faith is hanging in there when we are about to give it all up, and believing there is meaning and purpose when we can't see it at all. Faith is saying yes, there is someone much bigger than I whom I can trust, no matter what happens. That someone keeps repeating his promise: "If a person believes in me, even though he dies, he will live forever."

Faith, I don't even want to think what life would be without it.

📖 Fourth Sunday of Lent
(1 Sam 16:1b, 6-7, 10-13a; Eph 5:8-14; Jn 9: 1-41)

Our Gospel reading today is all about blindness and coming to see. Today I am going to talk about our blindness in matters of social justice and our blindness to the evils in our society. Our blindness makes us part of the problem without even realizing that we are.

Scripture tells us that God prefers justice in the world to our religious rituals. Our liturgy is important, but if our liturgy does not move us to work for social justice, something is wrong with our liturgy. God said through the prophet Amos, "I hate, I despise your feasts. I take no delight in your solemn assemblies, but let justice roll down like waters and righteousness like an ever-flowing stream."

Scripture tells us that God prefers justice to our asceticism, our penance, and our self-denial. God says through the prophet Isaiah, "Is this not the fast I choose: to loose the bonds of wickedness to undo the thongs of the yoke to let the oppressed go free and to break every yoke?"

When Matthew described the last judgment, people were not

to be judged on their religious practices, but on what they did or failed to do for the poor, the sick, and the imprisoned. In Luke's gospel, Jesus described his own ministry by announcing that he had come to proclaim release to the captives, recovery of sight to the blind, and liberty to the oppressed.

God says to us, "Get out of your own little world, you are part of a bigger world, a world of hurting people, a world where many do not have even basic human rights, a world full of injustice and repression, a world crying for justice and mercy."

The bishops of our Church have said that action on behalf of social justice is an essential dimension of the preaching of the Gospel. In other words, if we are not preaching social justice, we are not preaching the whole Gospel. The bishops have also said that the promotion of human rights is a requirement of the Gospel and must occupy a central position in our ministry.

We are products of our society and sometimes we are blind to the oppression and destruction that is part of that society. Most of the injustice and oppression comes from the structures of our society rather than from one individual hurting another. We get caught up in these structures and become a part of this social injustice without even realizing it and without consciously deciding to be part of it. We have no desire to hurt anyone. We have no bad will. We have not chosen to be oppressive; but still, because we cannot see, our actions and our lifestyle contribute to the destructiveness and reinforce the very structures that are hurtful.

Jesus came to give sight to the blind. He can help us to see. But we must first acknowledge our blindness if we want Jesus to heal it. Like the blind man at Jericho, we can call out to Jesus for help. Jesus asks us, "What do you want me to do for you?" We respond, "Lord, I want to see! I want to see the bigger world as you see it. I want to see the people as you see them."

📖 Fifth Sunday of Lent
(Ezek 37:12-14; Rom 8: 8-11; Jn 11: 1-45)

Today's Gospel is about death and resurrection. It's about dying into a new life that will never end. This particular reading contains the most important and startling conversation recorded in the Bible.

Jesus arrived in Bethany, a village less than two miles from Jerusalem. This is where his close friends: Martha, Mary, and Lazarus lived. Jesus was very close to them. He would go to their home for dinner and visiting. It was a place where Jesus could relax and let his hair down.

When Jesus heard that Lazarus had died, he cried. He waited a while then made his way to Bethany. Martha met Jesus right before he got there and said to him, "Lord, if you had been here my brother would never have died. Jesus answered Martha, "Your brother will rise again." Martha said, "I know he will rise again in the resurrection on the last day." But Jesus told her, "I am the resurrection and the life." Then Jesus continues, "Whoever believes in me, though he should die, will live forever." Then he asked Martha, "Do you believe what I just said? Do you believe me?" Martha answered, "Yes,

Lord, I have come to believe that you are the Messiah, the Son of God, he who is to come into the world."

This was a startling conversation because he was not just talking about Lazarus; he was talking about you and me. Jesus is promising us everlasting life because we believe in him. Jesus is promising that we will be resurrected into a whole new glorious state of being that will never end. We are asked to believe that our life on earth is the beginning of life that will continue forever.

Yes, we are mortal people. Yes, we will die. But as sad and tragic as death is, it is our only passageway to new life. Death is like a scary dark tunnel that we force ourselves to run through to get to the light at the end. Jesus says, "I am waiting for you at the end."

How would we answer Jesus today if he were to ask us what he asked Martha? "Do you believe this? Do you believe this about yourself? Do you believe I am talking about you and your future?" Precisely to the extent that we believe this, it will impact our lives, not only after death, but right now, today.

📖 Palm (Passion) Sunday
(Is 50:4-7; Phil 2:6-11; Mt 26:14-27, 66)

As we begin Holy Week today, we remember our redemption by Jesus Christ. To redeem means to "buy back at a cost," and we know what it cost Jesus Christ to buy us back from our sin.

There is a note of triumph in this Palm Sunday weekend. Jesus rides into Jerusalem with the crowds cheering him. He is their hero today, but he knows that won't last long. He knows the inconstancy of our hearts. He knows that the same people who cheer him today will be screaming for his blood next Friday.

I am reminded of the words of Fr. Michel Quoist, "Lord, it's too late for you to be quiet; you have spoken too much; you have fought too much. You were not sensible, you know, you exaggerated; it was bound to happen. You called the better people a breed of vipers. You told them that their hearts were black sepulchers with fine exteriors. You chose the decaying lepers. You are with notorious sinners, and you said that streetwalkers would be the first in paradise. You got on well with the poor, the bums, and the crippled. You belittled their religious regulations. Your interpretation of the law reduced it to one little commandment – to love. Now they are avenging themselves."[1]

We are invited to walk with Jesus through all of the events of this week. He invites us to join him for his last supper next Thursday. He invites us to his execution next Friday. He invites us to witness his glorious resurrection next Saturday evening and Sunday morning.

To accept Jesus' invitation will cost us something: some leisure time, some television shows, some computer game time, or something else. But have we already forgotten what it cost him to buy us back?

So his invitation is offered. May we not abandon him, but follow him…to the end.

---

[1] Michel Quoist, *Prayers*, (Sheed & Ward, 1963).

Holy Thursday
(Ex 12:1-8, 11-14; 1 Cor 11:23-26; Jn 13:1-15)

Jesus instituted the Eucharist, the greatest gift he has given us, the gift of himself. Then immediately he "…rose from the meal and took off his cloak. He picked up a towel and tied it around himself. Then he poured water into a basin and began to wash his disciples' feet…." They were amazed.

Wouldn't you think that after sharing the bread and passing the cup for the first time there would be a time of quiet, a time when the disciples would contemplate the depth of this miraculous meal? After all, we believe that when Jesus said to his disciples, "This is my body and this is my blood," the bread and wine become his body and blood. We believe that every time we do this together at Mass, in memory of him, the same thing happens. We believe that when we receive the Holy Eucharist, Jesus becomes present to us in a very special way. Yes, Jesus becomes one with us in every communion. But there is more. After the first Holy Eucharist, Jesus immediately washed their feet and said to them, "Do you understand what I just did for you? If I washed your feet, I who am teacher and Lord, then you must wash each other's feet. As I have done, so must you do."

The message is clear: Jesus gives himself to us in the Eucharist so that we may serve others as he did. Jesus was the man for others and he wants us to be the people for others. The Eucharist is not an end in itself. We do not receive Eucharist just to receive Eucharist. Our reception of Eucharist is supposed to do something for us. It should move us out of ourselves in practical, loving service to others.

I once read a newspaper account about an Italian cardinal who had died at ninety years of age. After his death they found that he had kept count of every Mass he had ever offered. From the day of his ordination, he counted every Mass through the 65 years of his priesthood. His final count was something like twenty-five thousand masses. I was edified by this story. I thought it showed a great devotion to the Mass, and surely, it did. But today I would ask a question. What did those Masses do for the cardinal? What does Mass do for you and me?

Jesus tells us that the Eucharist should lead us to loving service to others. If twenty-five thousand Masses lead us to twenty-five thousand acts of practical service to our neighbor, then the Eucharist is to us what it is meant to be. If it does not make us servants after the example of Jesus, then the Eucharist is not working.

Let us keep the words of Jesus in mind as we celebrate the

institution of the Eucharist, our greatest gift, but a gift that is not given for its own sake. The test of the Eucharist will be how we treat each other after the Mass.

Let us follow the example of Jesus at the Last Supper by washing the feet of our neighbors, that is, by serving them in myriad ways. Let us be a people who hear Jesus and act as real servants to others.

📖 Good Friday
(Is 52:13-53:12; Heb 4:14-16, 5:7-9; Jn 18:1-19:42)

During Holy week, Jesus lived the great mystery of his life. It was the mystery of how his totally unfair and apparently meaningless suffering and death led to resurrection and new life.

God is all-powerful and can arrange things anyway he wishes. Would not the incarnation, God's Son becoming man, be enough to save us? Would not his three years of preaching and healing have been enough? Why did God choose to save us by having his only Son nailed to a tree? Why did God, of all the possible ways of doing it, choose to put his Son through excruciating physical and emotional torment, drawing from him his last drop of blood, and his final sigh of hope? What father or mother would choose such a scenario for his or her child?

Pope John Paul II wrote about it in his book, *The Threshold of Hope.* He believed that the crucified Christ is proof of God's solidarity with us in our own suffering. The Cross, he believed is proof that God is always on the side of the suffering.

You and I live the same mystery in our lives. Today we see Jesus' death and resurrection. Jesus wants us to see ourselves in everything that happened to him. He wants us to recognize in our own lives the ways in which we have suffered as he suffered. He wants us to name our own physical and emotional pain, the hurts and agonies of our own life, whatever they may be. He wants us to ponder our own death that awaits us somewhere down the road.

Jesus was treated unfairly. He did not deserve such treatment. In our own lives we too have been treated unfairly, in ways we do not deserve. Jesus was treated with scorn and ridicule. In our own lives we know the pain of being disrespected, of not being taken seriously. Jesus was misunderstood. We too have lived with the pain of misunderstandings. We know the hurt of not being able to bring people to see the truth about us. Jesus died feeling lonely and abandoned. It was so devastating that he cried out, "My God, my God, why have you abandoned me?" We too know the suffering that comes with loneliness and abandonment. We cry out, "Can anybody see my pain? Does anyone care about me?" We know how much it hurts when we need people and they are not there for us.

Good Friday is not the end of Jesus' mystery, and our own suffering is not the end of our mystery. Jesus says, "Stay with me until Easter. I will show you how our suffering and death brings us to new life. Believe me. Trust me."

The scandal of the Cross remains. The mystery of suffering remains. But we know one thing for certain: when we suffer, we are not alone.

📖 Easter Sunday
(Acts 10:34a, 37-43; Col 3:1-4; Jn 20:1-9)

Today I want to tell you a true Easter story. It is about a woman in her mid 30's who was diagnosed with terminal cancer with three months to live. As she was getting her things in order, she asked her priest to visit her. She wanted to discuss certain aspects of her final wishes and to plan her funeral.

She told her priest which songs she wanted sung at her funeral service and she chose the scripture verses she wanted read. Her plans seemed to be in good order and the priest was about to leave when the young woman said, "Father, there's one more thing and this is really important. I want to be buried with a fork in my right hand." That stopped the priest in his tracks. "That surprises you, doesn't it," she asked. "Well, yes, to be honest, I'm more than a little puzzled by this request," he said. "Let me explain," she said. "From the time that I was a little girl, in all my years of attending church socials and potluck suppers, I remember that when the main course dishes were being cleared, my grandmother would lean over and say, 'Keep your fork.' It was my favorite part because I love desserts. I knew something better was coming, like chocolate cake or apple pie. So I want people to see me there in the casket with a fork in my hand. I want them to wonder, 'What's with the fork?' Then I want you to tell them, "Keep your fork, the best is yet to come."

She died and was laid out with the fork in her right hand. People asked over and over again, "What's with the fork?" and in his homily the priest told them about the fork and what it meant to her. Her simple faith in everlasting life spoke more powerfully than any homily could.

The message of Easter is simply this: Keep your fork, the best is yet to come. Jesus rose from the dead to a glorious new life; and Jesus is the firstborn from the dead. We will follow. We will rise to the same glorious new life. As Paul wrote in Ephesians 3, Jesus will give a new form to this lowly body of ours and remake it according to the pattern of his glorified body.

Easter is about the Resurrection of Jesus. Easter is about our own future resurrection. Can't you just picture the glorified, risen Jesus on this Easter Sunday morning, smiling on us and saying, "Keep your fork, the best is yet to come." Think of that every time you pick up your fork, and have a happy Easter.

📖 Second Sunday of Easter
(Acts 2:42-47; 1 Pt 1:3:9; Jn 20:19-31)

If you look in the dictionary under "D," you will find a listing for "Doubting Thomas." Today's gospel created this phrase in our language.

Do we fault Thomas for doubting? Picture this scene. Thomas knew Jesus had died. He knew he died nailed to a cross. Thomas knew Jesus was buried. He knew where he was buried. Thomas knew Jesus was really dead. So when his companions said to him, "We have seen the Lord," how would we expect him to react? How would we react?

Suppose you attended the funeral and burial of a friend. Then, later someone told you, "I just saw your friend." Wouldn't you react just like Thomas? "Sure you saw him. What do you take me for, a fool? When I see him and touch him to make sure he's real, then I'll believe."

Now here's where the stories take a different turn. Thomas got what he asked for. "Here I am, Thomas," said Jesus, touch me and do not be an unbeliever, but believe. You believe now because you have seen me. That's not difficult. Blessed are those who have not seen and believed."

Those people who have not seen, and yet have believed, are you and I. Jesus declared us blessed because we believe. Yes, we believe, and hopefully, we doubt too. Did you hear that right? Did I say that hopefully we doubt? Yes, and hopefully, I can explain what I mean.

The Easter season is all about faith. It is about faith in the resurrection of Jesus which we have not seen. It is about faith in our own resurrection to glorious new life which we have not seen or experienced. Do we really believe all this? "Yes, we say, I believe, but I wish I had some sign or proof that it is all true." Do we really believe in the resurrection of Jesus and in our own resurrection? "Yes, we say, but I cannot help but wonder, sometimes maybe even doubt. Does that mean I am losing my faith?"

No, my friends, it does not mean we are losing our faith. In fact, it means just the opposite. Our wonderment, our doubt is a sign that we do have faith. As one author put it, he who never doubted never half believed.

How could we not wonder and doubt? Do you ever look up into the night sky and wonder? Do you ever look at mountains, oceans, lightning, and clouds, and wonder? The God of the universe is too big to prove, too magnificent to nail down with certitude. So all we can do is wonder.

But because doubt is lonely and scary we build all kinds of protective walls and fences around our faith to make us feel secure. We lace our faith with all kinds of proofs and guarantees to make us feel secure. We want to be able to say, "Yes, I am certain. I am absolutely sure," because that feels better than the loneliness and fear of doubt. But the problem is that God and the resurrection and future eternal life are just too big to be fenced in.

I believe that our self-made guarantees actually hurt our faith; that our self-made certitude itself becomes the biggest lie; and that our certitude leaves little room for faith. Remember, faith is believing what we cannot see. Faith is believing what we cannot prove. When we are absolutely certain about something, we don't have to believe it.

Jesus said, blessed are those who have not seen, who are not certain, and have believed. He who never doubted, never half believed. In my years as a priest I have been with many people who were close to death. Never did anyone at that time say, "I am absolutely sure." So many did say, "Yes, I believe," and then they passed from faith to vision, into the arms of Jesus who said, "Blessed are those who have not seen and have believed."

📖 Third Sunday of Easter
(Acts 2:14, 22-33; 1 Pt 1:17-21; Lk 24:13-35)

Two disciples walked along the lonely road to Emmaus, their heads bowed, feeling dejected and depressed. They were discussing all that had happened in the last few days: a crucifixion, a burial, the crushing defeat of it all. They had left their fishing boats and had followed Jesus for three years. Certainly he was their long-awaited messiah. But then there came the crushing events of Holy Week. Their messiah was nailed to a cross like a common criminal. He died with people laughing at him, and he was buried in another man's tomb because he didn't have his own final resting place. It was all over.

Those three years had seemed so full of promise. They had hoped that he was the "one." But now it was over. They were wrong. What a crushing end to those years so full of hope. The Gospels tell us that Peter and the disciples went back to their fishing boats, back to the life they had known before Jesus, as if he had not been real.

Have you ever walked the road to Emmaus, looking at your own life, wondering where you are going, wondering if it really makes sense? We start off in youth with so many ambitions. We are so full of hopes and dreams for ourselves and our world. Then, the harsh reality sets in. Our life has become routine and dull. We may find ourself in a deadend job. Maybe our marriage has become difficult. We simply don't feel well. We feel burdened by the injustice and cruelty in the world. Our hopes and dreams become like sand castles on the beach, wiped away by the ocean waves.

Why were the two disciples so hopeless and disillusioned? Because they failed to recognize the one who walked with them. Why do we become hopeless and disillusioned? Because we fail to recognize the one who walks with us.

Jesus said to his disciples and to us, "Oh, how foolish you are. How slow of heart to believe." What is it that we are slow to believe? That Jesus is a real person, not an icon or just a person of past history. Jesus is risen, alive, and active! Jesus really does care for us, he really loves us, and he really is walking with us every step of the way.

Let's stop theologizing about Jesus. Sure, we know a lot of theology about him. He is the second person of the Holy Trinity, he is the Son of God who became man at Christmas, and he is truly divine and truly human, and so on. But have we theologized Jesus way up into the heavens, far away from us? We need to bring Jesus back. We need to make him real.

Let's use our imagination for a moment. Imagine the moment of your death. There you stand in brilliant light, and in the middle of the light stands Jesus, looking at you, smiling at you with outstretched arms. How do you react? "Oh my God, he's real!" And Jesus says to you, "Yes, I am real. I am your real friend, and I have been on the road with you every step of the way. Why did you not recognize me? It would have made such a difference."

The good news is that it is not too late. The road of life is sometimes wonderful and sometimes very hard; and what a difference it will make if we will only recognize Jesus along the way. What a difference when we remember that we never walk alone.

📖 Fourth Sunday of Easter
(Acts 2:14a, 36-41; 1 Pt 2:20b-25; Jn 10:1-10)

"I am the gate of the sheepfold." What in the world did Jesus mean by that? Picture the ancient sheepfold. It was a stone wall that formed a corral. There was an opening for the sheep to go in and out but no gate. At night, after herding his sheep into the corral, the good shepherd would then become the gate by lying down across the entrance. So when Jesus said, "I am the gate," he was saying that he would sacrifice his life for his sheep. He would place his very person between his sheep and any source of harm to them. Jesus way saying, "If you want to get to my sheep, you have to go through me first."

Why would Jesus give up his own life for us? He said, "I came so that they might have life and have it more abundantly." Do we hear that? Jesus wants us to live an abundant life. Do we? Each one of us has to think about that for himself or herself. I will tell you a few things that came to my mind when I reflected on this question.

1. An abundant life is big rather than small. How big is our world? We can limit it to small talk about our neighbors or enlarge it to include the world. How big or how small are

our concerns? I have known people who were really engaged in life, but then let their world get very small when they retired. Retirement does not mean non-engagement with life. Retirement offers new opportunities to enlarge our world. But retired or not, we need to ask ourselves if we are letting our world get small.

2. Living an abundant life means not settling for things as they are. Not getting stuck in the present, but welcoming new possibilities. It means not limiting ourselves to our present circumstances in life. It's so easy for us to say, "I can't do that because…"As George Bernard Shaw wrote, "People are always blaming their circumstances for what they are. I don't believe in circumstances. The people who get on with life are the people who look for the circumstances they want and, if they can't find them, they make them."

3. Living an abundant life means being engaged in life, not being merely spectators or bystanders. The former president of the Colombia University, Nicholas Murray Butler used to say that he divided the world into three classes: the few who make things happen, the many who watch things happen, and the vast majority, who have no idea of what happens. We need more people who make things happen.

Are we fully alive or half dead? Are we celebrating life or just tolerating it? When we wake up in the morning and look at the day ahead, do we see wonder, mystery, opportunity, and gift or does it look more like one darn thing after another? When we look at our basic life routines, what do they say to us? Do our habits of eating, drinking, and exercise make us feel alive or dead? How much time do we spend watching television, sitting in front of the computer, or playing video games? Do they enliven us or is it just passive escape from life? Do we find time each day to get in prayerful touch with ourselves, with God? Or do we play the game called, "I don't have time to pray." Prayer is absolutely necessary for an abundant life. The question, "Am I fully alive or half dead" becomes a spiritual question because Jesus said, "I came. I gave up my life that you might have life and have it more abundantly."

A woman was diagnosed as terminally ill. For a while she just continued to live pretty much as she always had. Then one day she asked herself, "What am I doing?" That day she decided to become fully engaged with life and to live life as it happens, one moment at a time. She lived 15 more months, but before she died, she told a friend, "The last 15 months were the best of my whole life."

Someone once wrote, "I pass through this world but once. Any good I can do, any kindness I can show to any human being, let me do it now, for I shall not pass this way again." Now that sounds like living an abundant life, the life Jesus wants for us.

📖 Fifth Sunday of Easter
(Acts 6:1-7; 1 Pt 2:4-9; Jn 14:1-12)

All I can say is thank you, Lord, for today's gospel. How often during the Easter Season we talk about the resurrection of Jesus and about his promise that we too will be resurrected to eternal life. Do we believe Jesus was raised from the dead to glorious new life? Our whole faith depends on that. Do we believe that we too will be raised to the same glorious new life? It sounds too good to be true, but we want to believe it. But Jesus does not want for us to just want to believe it. He wants us to believe it with our whole heart. He wants us to believe in our own resurrection as much as we believe in his.

So today Jesus brings this awesome and mysterious promise of resurrection right down to us in words we can understand. Listen to him: "Do not let your hearts be troubled. You have faith in God; have faith also in me. In my Father's house there are many dwelling places. If there were not would I have told you that I am going to prepare a place for you? And I will come back again and take you to myself, so that where I am you also may be." Listen to him.

Thank you, Lord, for this Gospel. How much clearer could

Jesus say it? He's preparing a place for you and me. Why? It is because he wants to take us to himself so that we can be together forever. Who can doubt his love for us? Who can doubt our own future resurrection? But we still wonder about it all.

Thank God for Thomas. He wondered too. Thomas said to Jesus, "Master, we do not know where you are going. How can we know the way?" Thomas was saying, this is all wonderful, but I still don't understand. I still have questions. Jesus answered him, "I am the way and the truth and the life." But we people are so insecure. We constantly look for assurances and guarantees. So thank God for Phillip. Phillip said to Jesus, "Show us the Father and that will be enough for us." Wow! Show us God the Father in all his Glory. Take us to heaven and show us your Father's house, then we can believe what you tell us with our whole heart. Jesus answered, "Have I been with you for so long and you still do not know me, Phillip? Whoever has seen me has seen the Father." Can Jesus give any more assurance?

This is a true story about Albert Einstein. He was riding a train and was very preoccupied with his work when the conductor stopped to punch his ticket. The great scientist began rummaging through his pockets, his briefcase, and looking all around somewhat bewildered because he couldn't find his ticket. "That's okay," the conductor told him, "We all know who you are, Dr. Einstein. I'm sure you bought a ticket. Don't worry about it." The conductor went on his way punching other tickets. Then he turned to see Dr. Einstein down on his hands and knees looking under the seat and around the floor. The conductor felt pity and walked back and said gently, "Dr. Einstein, please don't worry about it. I know who you are. Einstein looked up and said, "I know who I am too, what I don't know is where I am going."

This is not our story. We know where we are going. We are going to our place in our Father's house to be with God forever. We know the way. Jesus is our way. We have our destination. Our tickets have been punched. Of course we naturally wonder about it because we can't prove any of it. That's why Jesus asks us to believe him with our whole heart, and the more we believe him the bigger our hearts get. We are capable of loving God more. We are capable of loving each other more. We are capable of living life each day thanking and praising God as we stand in awe over the wonder of it all.

Sixth Sunday of Easter
(Acts 8:5-8, 14-17; 1Pt 3:15-18; Jn 14:15-21)

"If you love me, you will keep my commandments. Whoever has my commandments and observes them is the one who loves me." Another way of saying this is that actions speak louder than words. How true. If a child says, "I love you," but does not obey, instinctively parents react, "If you love me you will do as I say." Yes, actions speak louder than words.

In the parable of the two sons, the father said to the elder son, "Go and work in the vineyard." The son replied, "I am on my way, sir," but he never went. The father said the same thing to his second son. He answered, "No, I will not," but afterward regretted it and went. Jesus asked, "Which of the two did what the father wanted?" Yes, the second. Actions speak louder than words.

When I was a young boy I was watching a contractor build a house. He had finished a brick fireplace and had propped it up to keep it straight overnight. As he was leaving I was still standing there. He looked at me and said, "You wouldn't, would you?" I said, "Oh, I would never think of doing that."

He said, "I don't care what you think, just don't do it." Actions speak louder than words or thoughts.

I don't care how much we pray, how sweetly we talk to God or how warm and pious we feel, if we are not keeping God's commandments, it is all worthless. Worse, it is a lie because if we love God we will keep his commandments. That's the test. Why do we keep the commandments? Jesus said, "Keep my commandments because you love me." Is this why we keep them?

There is an old legend about an angel walking down the street carrying a torch in one hand and a pail of water in the other. Someone asked the angel what he was doing with those. The angel replied, "With the torch I am going to burn down the mansions of heaven. With the pail of water I'm going to put out the fires of hell. I'm going to erase heaven and hell, and then we shall see who really loves God.

Do we keep the commandments more out of fear of punishment or hope of reward than out of love of God? Well, you might say, what difference does it make as long as we keep them? What difference? It makes all the difference in the world. It's a difference between a child who does his chores because he loves his parents or because they will pay him to do it or punish him if he doesn't. It's the difference between saying to God, "I will obey you because I'm afraid what you will do to me if I don't," or "I obey you God because I love you."

Scripture has a lot of references to heaven and hell, reward and punishment, but Scripture has a lot more references to love. God wants our whole-hearted love. Sure, there may be times when only the fear of punishment and hope of reward keep us on track. That's okay at times. But God does not want us to live our lives that way. God wants our obedience from love.

God so loved the world that he sent his only son. His only son loves us so much that he died for us. Do you want to know who you really love? Make a list of those people you would actually die for. It will be a short list and they will be people very special to you. That's how special we are to God.

What does God ask of us in return? If you love me, you will keep my commandments. Whoever has my commandments and observes them is the one who loves me.

📖 Seventh Sunday of Easter
(Acts 1:12-14; 1 Pt 4:13-16; Jn 17:1-11a)

How many of us believe Jesus wants us to be truly holy people? How many of us want to be truly holy people? I was speaking recently with a woman about her spiritual life. She said what probably most of us could say. She said, "I don't seem to be going anywhere. I find myself constantly slipping back into my old ways and faults. I don't seem to change. I don't seem to be getting any better." I'll bet we all feel this way to some degree or another.

Today, I want to give you and myself the ultimate spiritual challenge. As with any challenge, we are free to embrace it or reject it. Today I challenge you and myself to stop treading water and start swimming in the spiritual life. I challenge us to take the risk of changing rather than settling for who we are now. I challenge us to make the serious decision to become the full person God wants us to be. Now that might all sound good, but do we really want it?

This is the blessed time for such a challenge. We are now in the time between the ascension of Jesus into heaven and Pentecost which we celebrate next Sunday. Our first reading tells us how the disciples spent the nine days between Ascension Thursday and Pentecost Sunday. In the upstairs room they devoted themselves to constant prayer. A novena is nine days of special prayer. So we can say the disciples made the first novena in anticipation of the gift of the Holy Spirit Jesus had promised them.

What is Pentecost? It is the celebration of God, the Holy Spirit. Who is the Holy Spirit? The Holy Spirit empowers us to grow and sanctifies us and makes us holy because we cannot make ourselves holy.

In all truth we do get bogged down spiritually. We don't even know what to do to get moving. We may have some fantasy about what we will be like when we are really holy, but, we don't even know what holiness looks like. That's why we have the Holy Spirit. The Holy Spirit knows what we need and how we must change to become those fully-alive people God wants us to be. The Holy Spirit can and will do it if we want it to happen.

That's the big question. Do we want the Holy Spirit? Do we want to be holy? Don't say yes too quickly. This is worth thinking about. When we think of holiness do we think of gift, fullness, and joy or do we think of deprivation and suffering? If the Holy Spirit makes us holy, will the Spirit fill us with everything good or will the Spirit deprive us of what we treasure?

That's why we need to think about what we really want. Since we don't know what it will take to make us holy, obviously there is some risk involved. When we are faced with risk we need corresponding trust. Do we choose to trust God and take that risk or do we prefer to leave things alone and settle for ourselves the way we are?

Today I offer you and myself the ultimate spiritual challenge. I challenge us to be like the disciples, to pray especially hard over the week ahead that the Holy Spirit will come to us and do whatever it takes to make us holy people.

Now, I issue a warning: don't pray for it unless you really want it. Jesus promised us this is the one prayer that will certainly be answered. "The Father in heaven will give the Holy Spirit to those who ask him" (Lk 11:13). "I give you my assurance. Whatever you ask the Spirit will give you." This week could be the most important time of the year. Do we want it to be? Will we take that leap of faith and trust?

📖 Ascension
(Acts 1:1-11; Eph 1:17-23; Mt 28:16-20)

The feast of Ascension is the feast of Jesus returning to his Father in heaven. He had finished his work on earth. He taught us the good news about our God and God's love for us. He validated that truth with his saving death on the cross and his resurrection to glorious new life. Now it was time to return to his Father. This may sound like an ending, but it is really a beginning, the beginning of something truly miraculous.

What did Jesus leave behind? He left a small group of followers. And what an unlikely group it was. In our first reading those disciples asked him, "Lord, are you at this time going to restore the kingdom to Israel?" Can you believe that? After all this time, after the events of Good Friday and Easter Sunday, they still did not get the message? They were still looking for him to be the powerful messiah who would restore Israel to its former glory. Can't you see Jesus shake his head in disbelief?

And our gospel seems even more curious. When the disciples saw Jesus they worshipped, but they doubted. How could they worship and doubt at the same time? As Jesus spent his final moments on earth, his closest followers were still not sure. "Jesus, are you sure this is the time to leave?" Now let's continue this curious scene. What does Jesus do? He doesn't throw up his hands in despair. He does just the opposite. He tells them, "You will be my witnesses in Jerusalem, throughout Judea and Samaria and to the ends of the earth. Go, therefore and make disciples of all the nations." To the ends of the earth? To all nations? Jesus never traveled 100 miles from the place he was born. Now he is commissioning these disciples, who are slow to understand and still doubt, to bring his good news to the whole world.

Now let's pause for a moment to keep this in perspective. If you were a betting person, what odds would you ask to bet it would succeed: one hundred to one, one million to one? No thanks. If you were an investor, how much of your hard-earned money would you invest in this worldwide enterprise? "Jesus, are you sure it's time for you to leave?"

Jesus knew what he was doing. Besides, he was not really leaving. "Behold, I am with you always." And even more, Jesus assured them that, "In a few days you will be baptized with the Holy Spirit. You will receive power when the Holy Spirit comes upon you." And all that happened in a few days. We celebrate all that happening next Sunday which is Pentecost.

And look what the Holy Spirit did with the disciples on Pentecost. And look what has happened over the past 2,000 years. What looked like certain failure actually brought the good news of Jesus to the ends of the earth. And it is not over. We are Jesus' disciples in our world today. Our world today needs the good news as much as it ever did. And now it is up to us to continue this mission. Up to us? Right! Sure we are just like the first disciples: slow to understand and full of doubt. But just like the Holy Spirit empowered them, Jesus promised us the same Holy Spirit. The same Holy Spirit empowers us to spread the good news by our words and our lives.

Next Sunday is our Pentecost. Next Sunday we will celebrate our own giftedness and empowerment in the Holy Spirit. So, people, why are you standing there looking at the sky? With joy and courage we will be his witnesses in our homes, our neighborhoods, and in our workplaces. Pope John XXIII wrote, "Every believer in this world must become a spark of light." Let us sparkle!

📖 Pentecost
(Acts 2:1-11; 1 Cor 12:3b-7, 12-13; Jn 20:19-23)

Pentecost is a spectacular feast. Spectacular means: marvelous, breathtaking, stunning, dazzling, extraordinary, awesome. Pentecost is a spectacular feast. How many of us live spectacular lives? That's why we tend to think of Pentecost as someone else's celebration or gift. And we say, "Wow! What an experience that must have been." Again, it is someone else's experience.

Jesus promised us the same Holy Spirit who empowered and transformed those disciples in the upper room. Did Jesus really mean it? Of course he did. Jesus was not joking. Then why don't we experience the Holy Spirit in our lives? We do! I'm not talking about spectacular phenomena like rushing wind and fire. Our God is not a flashy God. God does not usually do showy things to get our attention. God deals with us in ordinary ways, in the ordinary circumstances of our daily lives. Yes, Jesus kept his promise. The Holy Spirit is here if we will but recognize the Spirit.

In the second reading Paul says that no one can say "Jesus is Lord" except in the Holy Spirit. No one can pray except in the Holy Spirit. I want all of us together to say, "Jesus is Lord." I want us to say it because we mean it and believe it. Together now, JESUS IS LORD! Now that may not have sounded spectacular, but there is something special and wonderful about hundreds of people, united in faith, praying the name of Jesus and meaning it. What we just said we were able to say because of the Holy Spirit.

Did Jesus mean it when he promised to give us this same Holy Spirit? Let's look at our lives. No mother ever stayed up all night in concern for her child except in the Holy Spirit. We have never reached out to another in real care except in the Holy Spirit. We have never tried to make another happy except in the Holy Spirit. We have never held on through difficult times except in the Holy Spirit.

Is the Holy Spirit active in our lives? Remember that time you were more patient than you dreamed possible. Remember that time you had the courage to say something and your courage surprised you. Remember that situation when you simply acted bigger than yourself, and you knew it. Remember when love moved you to tears. Remember when you felt totally alive and your whole being was filled with life and all you could say was "God is good." Is the Holy Spirit active in our lives? Did Jesus keep his promise?

We live and breathe and move and have our being in the

Holy Spirit. Recognize the Spirit in you. Welcome and converse with the Spirit in you. As our friendship with the Spirit grows, so will the power of the Spirit grow in us. There is something spectacular about that. Pentecost is not someone else's feast, it is ours.

📖 Trinity Sunday
(Ex 34:4b-6; 2 Cor 13:11-13; Jn 3)

Religion is full of mystery. It has to be because religion is about our relationship with God, and God is a mystery. We deal constantly with mystery. Life is mystery. Resurrection and eternal life are mystery. No wonder Jesus said over and over again, "Believe me, trust me, have faith in me and in what I tell you."

Well, if we ever needed faith, it is today. Today is Trinity Sunday. Some of us are old enough to remember learning our faith from the Baltimore Catechism. Question 23 was: what do we mean by the Blessed Trinity? Answer: By the Blessed Trinity we mean one and the same God in three divine persons, the Father, Son, and the Holy Spirit. Now would someone like to explain that to me?

For two thousand years theologians have tried to find the words to say something about the Trinity. Here is an example. From all eternity God the Father sees and knows Himself. In knowing Himself he utters a Word. This Word is the expression of who God is. This Word is the Second Person of the Trinity, God the Son, the Word who was made flesh in Jesus. As the Father knows the Son and the Son knows the Father, the love they have for each other is the Holy Spirit.

The mystery of the Trinity is that pure being, pure truth, and pure love exist in God as three distinct persons. Now, does that help us or do we feel like saying, "Run that by me again, will you?" If there is ever a day to know the meaning of faith, believing what we cannot understand, it is today. We do believe and we express our faith in many ways. We begin each Mass with the sign of the cross: in the name of the Father, Son, and Holy Spirit. We end each Mass with the blessing of the Father, Son, and Holy Spirit. A lot of baseball players express their faith when they come to bat, although it's a pretty quick act of faith.

So in truth and humility, we stand before God today and say, "I don't understand you, Lord. You are simply too much for me to comprehend. But I love you God. How can we love someone whom we don't understand? How can we love a mystery? We can because God has told us enough about Himself and we are drawn to God in love.

Listen to today's readings. In Exodus we read that God describes Himself to Moses. He is the Lord, a merciful, gracious God; slow to anger and rich in kindness. In second Corinthians we read that the God of love and peace is with you. In John we learn that God so loved the world that he gave His only Son. God did not send His Son into the world to condemn the world but that the world might be saved through him.

Listen to these key words about God: merciful, gracious, slow to anger, rich in kindness, love, peace, salvation, not condemnation. We have all this about God in just three readings today. Every mass we hear more about God's unconditional love for us. How can we love one we cannot understand? This is the wrong question. The right question is: how can we not love a God like this? Yes Lord, we believe. So let's stop making the sign of the cross out of routine and habit. Let's make every sign of the cross a real act of faith in the Father, Son, and Holy Spirit.

📖 Corpus Christi
(Dt 8:2-3, 14b-16a; 1 Cor 10:16-17; Jn 6:51-58)

I believe that the Gospel of John contains the most extraordinary of all Jesus' teachings. "I am the living bread that came down from heaven," said Jesus. "And the bread I will give is my flesh for the life of the world." The Jews quarreled among themselves, "How can this man give us his flesh to eat?" That was a very reasonable question. They were saying, "What are you talking about, Jesus. This is preposterous. How can you make bread into your flesh? You must have a hidden meaning here, Jesus. You can't really mean that."

Does Jesus back off? He responds, "Amen, amen, I say to you. Whoever eats my flesh and drinks my blood has eternal life. For my flesh is true food; and my blood is true drink. Many of his disciples remarked, "This sort of talk is hard to endure. How can anyone take it seriously?" That is another good question. This is tough stuff, Jesus. You are asking a lot if you want us to take you seriously. And besides, why in the world would you want us to eat your flesh and drink your blood?

Jesus tells us why. "Whoever eats my flesh and drinks my blood remains in me and I in him. The one who feeds on me will have life because of me." As John's gospel tells us, many of Jesus' disciples broke away and would not remain in his company any longer. "Jesus, you are alienating a lot of people. You are losing your following. Now is the time to tell us you don't really mean it, that you are not serious."

What does Jesus do? He said this to the twelve, "Do you want to leave me too?" He told them in essence that he was completely serious and that he meant what he said even if it meant losing them also. Simon Peter answered, "Lord, to whom shall we go? You have the words of eternal life."

Again, in truth and humility we stand before the Lord and say, Lord, we don't understand you. How can you give us yourself in this Eucharistic bread and wine? I think Jesus would respond, "You don't understand and you can't understand, but God can do anything He wants." So Jesus, what you promised in today's gospels, what you did at the Last Supper, what your Church has been doing at every mass since, is it actually true? "Yes," Jesus responds. "What I promised is true. What I did was true. What you do today is true. Whoever receives the Holy Eucharist receives me and will remain in me and I in him. And whoever eats this bread will live forever."

I was talking with a couple the other day. They told me that the sermons at their church were so bad that they started attending a Protestant church. The sermons were better there, but before long they started missing something. Something was not there. Then they realized that there was no Holy Eucharist there. So they came back to their church in spite of the poor sermons.

My point is not to justify bad sermons, but to speak to the emptiness we would feel if we were deprived of union with Jesus in the Holy Eucharist. "Oh, but Mass is so boring." Ever heard that? Once when I was speaking to a young relative who did not go to Mass very often, she gave me her reasons. "Mass is so boring and I don't get anything out of it," she said. "I pray, but I like to pray outdoors, in the mountains, looking at a sunset." I told her that was good, but then I told her that Mass was not in competition with MTV or NASCAR or any form of entertainment. I told her we are dealing with something much more important than entertainment. I asked her if she believed in the presence of Jesus in the Holy Eucharist. She said she did. "Well, if you do," I told her, "how can you say you get nothing out of Mass? If you believe, how can you possibly stay away?"

Yes, Lord, we believe you. We do not understand how, but, like Peter, we believe that you have the words of eternal life. That's why we are here again today.

📖 Tenth Sunday of the Year
(Hos 6:3-6; Rom 4:18-25; Mt 9:9-13)

Today's Gospel is about Jesus and sinners. So all of us who know we are sinners can say, "Thank you, Lord, for today's Gospel." If you do not see yourself as a sinner, you may take a nap for the next few minutes because our Gospel has nothing to do with you. Okay, fellow sinners, let's get in touch with the real power of this Gospel. Let's see what Jesus really thinks about sinners like you and me.

Jesus saw Matthew sitting at his customs post. Matthew is not an ordinary sinner. He gets a trophy for his sinful life. Matthew was then the chief tax collector, who dunned his fellow Jews for their money. He took his percentage and turned the rest over to those hated Romans to support their troops who occupied Israel. His sin was greed, dishonesty, betrayal, injustice, oppression, you name it. Matthew was well known by the people and despised for what he was doing to them. Yet, this was the man whom Jesus singled out and invited to "Follow me." Jesus did not say, "Shame on you for what you've done. He said, "Follow me." Jesus did not say, "Once you get your act together, give me a call." He said, "Follow me." Without any judgment or condemnation, Jesus said, "Follow me."

Now that's enough to raise some eyebrows, but there is more. Jesus had dinner with Matthew and many tax collectors and sinners. In the Jewish culture eating together was the most intimate thing you could do with a friend. Breaking bread together was a sign of affection and communion with one's guests. It was a way of saying, "I think a lot of you, and I love you."

Are we getting the picture? The Pharisees, who were the righteous ones, saw this dinner party and asked the disciples, "Why does your teacher eat with the tax collectors and the sinners?" They thought, "This is scandalous, Jesus, what are you doing? What are you thinking?" Jesus told them what he was thinking. "Those who are well do not need a physician, the sick do. Go and learn the meaning of the words, 'I desire mercy, not sacrifice.' I did not come to call the righteous, but the sinners."

Do we hear Jesus? If we do, which one of can say, "But Lord, I am so sinful that I am not worthy to be close to you." Of course we are not worthy. But Jesus did not come for the worthy, but for the unworthy. He forgives us and wants us to be close to him. "But Lord, I have been so bad that I don't see how you can really forgive me." Do we think that our sin is greater than God's mercy?

There is not a hopeless one among us, no matter what we have done. G.K. Chesterton might have had today's Gospel in mind when he wrote, "Love means to love the unlovable. Hope means hoping when things seem hopeless."

Jesus gives us that love, that forgiveness, and that hope. Which one of us can say no to that? Jesus says to you and me, "Follow me." Which one of us can say no to that? Thank you Lord, you came for sinners, for us.

📖 Eleventh Sunday of the Year
(Ex 19:2-6a; Rom 5:6-11; Mt 9:36-10:8)

"At the sight of the crowds Jesus was moved with compassion for them because they were troubled and abandoned, like sheep without a shepherd."

As we look around, do you think Jesus might be talking about us today? Are there crowds today that look troubled and abandoned, like sheep without a shepherd? Are there crowds today that seem to be wandering aimlessly through life, not rooted in anything of purpose or value? And why are these crowds not looking to the churches for direction, guidance, and purpose? Why do so many find that church is not relevant in their lives? Have we lost our focus so that we are no longer looked upon as shepherds and leaders?

Do you ever read the comic strip Doonesbury by Gary Trudeau? He likes to be somewhat irreverent and occasionally he takes us to his little church at Walden. The pastor is Rev. Scot who is struggling to make his church relevant and meaningful. One Sunday Pastor Scot is making his announcements. "Okay, flock, I'll run through this week's activities: This Monday we have a lecture on nutrition from

Kate Moss' personal chef. Tuesday and Thursday will be our regular 12-step nights. Friday at 6:30 p.m. is our organic gardening workshop. Saturday night will be aerobic male bonding night, so bring your sneakers. Are there any questions?" A voice comes from the back of the church, "Is there a church service this week?" Without a pause, Scot says, "Cancelled. There was a conflict with the self-esteem workshop."

We are surrounded by experts and gurus who offer all kinds of advice on how to feel better about ourselves and how to cope with life, who think they can fill the emptiness inside. But the crowds still look troubled and abandoned, like sheep without a shepherd. I think our television shows mirror quite well the emptiness, futility, and vanity that is so rampant among us. Do you really care who Donald Trump hires or fires? God save us. In another show, "Do you want to be a Hilton?" Paris Hilton's mother is taking a group of diamonds in the rough and will polish them to be just like Paris. God save us.

We need to refocus and our focus is on Jesus. Has Jesus lost his relevance in our world today? No way! Jesus has been relevant for 2,000 years and will be relevant forever. A friend of mine asked me an interesting question recently. She is not a believer, at least in organized religion. She asked me, "If you could go back in time for a little while, what era would you choose?" As I was thinking about that, she said, "I would go back to the time of Jesus, even though I don't believe he is God. I would want to see and hear his love which must be fantastic."

Why is Jesus relevant? He is relevant because he looked on people with compassion and love. And we do not have to worry about being relevant if we do the same. Jesus did not make religion complicated. We have done that. Jesus made it just as simple as, "Love one another as I have loved you." That is our focus. Just love one another as Jesus loves us. Start with the people closest to you, your family, friends, and co-workers. Then, let your love reach others, the hungry, the naked, the sick, and the imprisoned.

If we would just focus on being loving people, we don't have to worry about anything else, because loving one another *is* loving God. And since God is love, God is found in everything loving about us.

These crowds of wandering sheep without a shepherd will be touched by the love and compassion of God through us if we will just stay focused.

Twelfth Sunday of the Year
(Jer 20:10-13; Rom 5:12-15; Mt 10: 26-33)

Jesus said, "Fear no one. Do not be afraid." Do we live with too much fear and anxiety? We are not talking about fear of real danger. Fear is a valuable human emotion. If a truck is bearing down on us fear will make us get out of the way. So what does Jesus mean when he tells us not to be afraid? He said, "Fear no one." He is talking about people. Are we afraid of people? Are we afraid of God?

Are we afraid to try some things because we are afraid of making a mistake, of being laughed at and ridiculed? Are we afraid of what people think of us? How much of our self-worth depends on other people? Does their approval make us feel worthwhile? Does their disapproval make us think less of ourselves? I suppose we all will answer yes to these questions to one extent or another. But the more we look to people for our own self-worth, the more we fear people and what they can do to us.

Are we afraid of God? Oh, but doesn't the Bible tell us to fear God? The Book of Proverbs says, "Fear of the Lord is the beginning of wisdom." Yes, the Bible does speak a lot about fear of the Lord, but that is reverential fear. It means always holding God in complete awe and reverence because God is awesome. But that is very different from fear that makes us anxious or that paralyzes our relationship to God.

Are we afraid of God? Fear of God can show itself in our fear of becoming too holy because that might mean more suffering for us. It can show itself in our fear of God's will because that usually means something tough. It can show itself in our fear of giving ourselves completely to God because of what God may ask of us. "God, I wish you would cooperate more with my plans because – and this is hard to say but it is honest – I trust my own plan for me more than I trust your plan for me."

Why is fear of people and God so important that Jesus cautions us against it in today's gospel? The whole message of Jesus is to love God and one another with our whole heart. And think about this, we cannot love someone of whom we are afraid. If we are afraid of God, we cannot really love God. If we are afraid of a person, we cannot really love that person. No wonder Jesus said, "Fear no one," because that fear gets in the way of loving them.

Why should we not fear anyone, including God? In today's gospel Jesus tells us why in words that cannot be improved on. Listen. "Are not two sparrows sold for a small coin? Yet, not one of them falls to the ground without your Father's knowledge." Do we believe that? Do we believe that God is so aware of all his creation that a bird does not fall to the ground without his knowing it? Keep listening. "Even all the hairs of your head are counted." Do we believe that? Do we believe that God knows each one of us so well? God is concerned with each one of us that he has counted the number of hairs on our heads? Keep listening. "So do not be afraid. You are worth more than many sparrows." You and I are worth so much to God. Simply put, fear no one.

📖 Thirteenth Sunday of the Year
(2 Kgs 4:8-11, 14-16a; Rom 3:6-4, 8-11; Mt 10:37-42)

"Whoever loves father, mother, son, daughter more than me is not worthy of me." At first glance, that sounds a little harsh. But Jesus is not saying that we should not love our family members. He wants us to love them just as he loves us. What he is saying is that he must always be first in our lives. If we choose to follow Jesus we must love him and be dedicated to him so much that even our closest loved ones will never get in the way of our total dedication to Jesus. This is not an either/or situation. It is both/and. Because the more we love Jesus, the more we will love other people.

Jesus says, "Whoever does not take up his cross and follow me is not worthy of me." He is not saying, "If you choose to follow me I will make you suffer." Everyone, Christian and non Christian alike, lives with a certain measure of suffering. There is no such thing as a pain-free life. When Jesus asks us to take up our cross, he invites us to see our cross as more than unavoidable suffering.

Suffering is a mystery that we cannot fully understand. Why did Jesus suffer so to redeem us? But we know his suffering redeemed the world. When we join our suffering to his rather than just tolerating it, in some way our suffering becomes redeeming for us and others too. It makes a huge difference whether we take up our cross in faith or just drag our cross. Besides, it's a lot heavier when we drag it.

Can good come from our suffering as it came from Jesus' suffering? Why else would Helen Keller write, "I thank God for my blindness, for through it I have found myself, my work, and my God."?

"Whoever finds his life will lose it, and whoever loses his life for my sake will find it." I like even better the earlier translation of this statement, "He who seeks only himself brings himself to ruin, whereas he who brings himself to nothing for me discovers who he is." Jesus is giving us the key to self discovery and happiness. We all want to be happy. So let's find the key.

We are born into this world self-centered and self-absorbed babies concerned about ourselves. Our lifelong struggle is to move away from being so self-centered and self-seeking. Jesus shows us how. He is the model of who we can be. Jesus is called "the man for others." His whole life was given in service to others. His whole orientation was opposite of our self-centeredness. Jesus tells us his way is our way. His way will bring us to self-discovery and happiness.

Is Jesus saying that it is in forgetting self that we find self, and that it is in losing our life that we find it? Exactly, and our own experience bears this out. The more we seek our own happiness, the less happy we are. The more we are focused inwardly on ourselves, the more miserable we become. The more we forget about making ourselves happy, the happier we become. The more we become concerned with the happiness of others, the more we experience joy and fulfillment.

At first glance it does not seem to make good sense. It should be the other way around. But our own experience proves that it is true. Our most unhappy times have been when we turned in on ourselves, we were concerned only about ourselves, and we made ourselves and our needs the center of our attention. Our happiest times are those when we forget ourselves in love and service to others.

What profound truth in this one statement by Jesus. It is a profound truth that holds the key to our happiness. Jesus has given us the key. Now it is up to you and me to use this key.

📖 Fourteenth Sunday of the Year
(Zec 9:9-10; Rom 8:9, 11-13; Mt 11:25-30)

Today let us look at our religious perspective and practice. Is there anyone of you who feels burdened by religion? Is there anyone of you who feels like your religion is so heavy and complicated that it is hard to meet all the demands on you? Well listen to Jesus in today's Gospel. "Come to me all you who labor and are burdened and I will give you rest." Do we hear that? Oh, that sounds wonderful. Ah, sweet rest. Who could refuse such an invitation?

But wait! Jesus is not finished. "Take my yoke upon you and learn from me and you will find rest for yourselves. For my yoke is easy and my burden light." Now just a minute. What's this stuff about a yoke? A yoke was a wooden platform that fit around the neck and rested on the shoulders. People used it to carry food, jugs of water, and whatever else they needed to carry. And Jesus says, "Take my yoke upon you. My yoke is not heavy. It fits you well. It rests lightly on your shoulders." Now wait a minute, Jesus. Are you saying that following you is easy? Easy compared to what? Jesus is comparing his yoke to the yoke of the Pharisees. The Pharisees burdened people with all their laws and regulations and Jesus condemned them for doing this. They tie up heavy burdens and lay them on people's shoulders but will not lift a finger to lighten them. The Pharisees piled more than 600 laws on their yoke. It caused people to labor and be burdened as they tried to keep up with all the laws.

Jesus said, "My yoke is easy and my burden light." What is your yoke, Jesus? Picture the scene at the Last Supper on Thursday night. Listen to Jesus' final words to his followers. Final words are like a last will and testament. They take on a special importance. Let's open his will and see what Jesus leaves us with. "My one commandment is to love one another as I have loved you. I tell you this that my joy may be yours, and your joy may be complete. Again I say, love one another as I have loved you." Signed, Jesus Christ. Jesus puts one law on our yoke, the law of love.

Our question today is: Whose yoke are we carrying? When we examine our religious practice, are we carrying the yoke of the Pharisees, heavy with law, or the yoke of Jesus, focused on love?

I was discussing this with a man who found that trying to be a good Christian took all the fun out of his life. "All these commandments and rules are heavy and serious stuff," he said, "and confusing, Father." He wanted his load lightened.

He said, "You tell me what is right and wrong, what is a sin, and I will do exactly as you tell me. Then, when I die, if I find out it is wrong, it will be your fault, not mine." He had a heavy load.

When I was at another parish a woman whose religion was so heavy and legalistic that she drove both of her daughters from the church, left the parish because she thought that I was "too liberal. " I did not see her for five years until one day after a Sunday Mass. I saw her coming up the sidewalk directly to me. Oh boy, I thought, what have I done wrong now? She told me she had six weeks to live and asked if I could be with her through the last weeks. We talked a lot. Then she looked me in the eye and said, "Father, you think I have been all wrong, don't you?" How could I answer that to a woman who may have one week to live? I told her, "Gerrie, you know we don't agree in many ways. But I know Jesus loves you. And I know you have lived your life consistently as you thought you should. I hope someone can say that about me." And I said that at her funeral a few days later. She had lived with a very heavy load.

How about us? Whose yoke are we carrying? I am not saying church law is unimportant. Law is like the structure of a skeleton which holds the whole body together. But church law was never intended to be the heart and life blood of our religion. Jesus gave us his one commandment. And if we take that on our shoulders, we will find rest, for his yoke is easy and his burden light.

📖 Fifteenth Sunday of the Year
(Is 55:10-11; Rom 8:18-23; Mt 13:1-9)

"My Word that goes forth from my mouth shall not return to me void but shall do my will achieving the end for which I sent it." Now that sounds powerful, doesn't it? How powerful is it to you and me? We hear God's word every time we come to mass. Have we taken the Word into ourselves? Another way of asking this is, what difference has it made? How has God's Word changed us?

A Protestant church hired a new pastor. Members of the church anxiously awaited his first sermon. He preached eloquently. Everyone was pleased. The next Sunday they returned, anxious to hear him again. They were totally shocked when he repeated the same sermon word for word. After the services they asked him, "Don't you know what you did? Don't you know that you gave us the same sermon as last week?" "Yes," he told them, "I know that, and I shall continue giving the same sermon week after week until I see some action and change, until I see you do something about what I am saying." If I tried that, how long before you threw me out?

In our Gospel there is nothing wrong with God's Word. God sows good seed. But the best of seed needs good soil. We are the soil. Today is a gut-check for you and me to see what kind of soil we are. We can be a footpath with little soil. We just are not excited or interested in God's Word. It becomes old hat. The more traveled a footpath, the harder it becomes. The footpath of our mind is very well traveled. We live with a constant flow of traffic: audio visual stimuli, TV, movies, video games, lots of traffic that can harden us to God's Word. The expression we might use to describe this soil: it goes in one ear and out the other.

We can be rocky ground so that God's Word cannot take root in us. How can we be rocky ground? Can we have our minds already made up so that God can't get through to us? Do we have it already figured out for ourselves, so set with our own plans, that we see no need to change? Is God speaking to rock? Our expression to describe this soil is: it's like talking to a wall.

We can be living among thorns which choke off God's Word. Do we have thorns in our lives that are competing with God's Word? Do we have some attachments, activities, relationships that must be rooted out for God's Word to take hold? Are we living compromised in some way that is contrary to God's Word? An expression to describe this soil might be: You don't listen to me because you are afraid to hear what I may say.

Now where are you, where am I in this Gospel? Can we see ourselves in the footpath, rocky ground, among the thorns? How can we know what kind of soil we are? Quite easily! Something should be happening with us. We cannot just stay the same people. I suggest a few questions for each of us to reflect on. Am I the same person I was five years ago? How have I changed? How am I different? Are my values, what is most important to me, different from five years ago? Has my perspective, the way I see God, the way I see life, the way I see myself changed over these five years?

If any of us say no to all of this, then God's Word has not achieved the end for which it was sent. But if we see real differences in us from five years ago, then we are the rich soil, we are the ones who have heard and understood, and who have put God's Word into action, bearing fruit in our lives and the lives of others. It's worth thinking about because God is not through speaking to us. God will keep speaking each week because God wants us to take root and grow into those beautiful people God calls us to be.

📖 Sixteenth Sunday of the Year
(Wis 12:13, 16-19; Rom 8:26-27; Mt 13:24-30)

In last week's gospel Jesus gave us a parable about sowing seed on different kinds of soil. A parable is a short story with a message or teaching. Today Jesus gives us another one. Notice again the agricultural theme. All of his parables are very earthy and easy for the people of his day to relate to.

The beauty and power of the parable is that there is always more to it than meets the eye. Parables can be read in different ways to teach us different truths. But today's parable is one of just a couple in which Jesus actually tells us the meaning. The farmer, who is God, sowed good seed in his field. At night an enemy, who is the devil, sneaked in and scattered weeds through his whole crop. As the crop grew, so did the weeds, all mixed up with the wheat. What a mess. The farmer's helpers asked him, "Do you want us to go and pull them up?" "No," he replied, "let them grow together until harvest."

What is the message of this parable? It is about the existence of evil in our world and about God's tolerance of evil. The wheat is the good folks choosing to be loving and caring people. The weeds are the evil doers, those people who choose to hurt rather than love. When we are both living together in the same world it gets pretty messy. So the helpers are anxious to get rid of the weeds and to clean up the whole mess. They ask, "Do you want us to pull them up?" Aren't we just like them? When we see all the evil in our world don't we think thoughts like, "How can God allow so much evil?" "How can God stand this if he is so good?" "Why doesn't God do something about this?" "God, why don't you pull them up?" But wait a minute. Before we get too frustrated with God over the evil in our world, we need to pause and think about ourselves. Aren't we glad that God is patient with us rather than pulling us up right after some of the bad choices we have made?

In the parable, God said, "No, let them grow together until harvest. Then I shall separate the good from the bad." Why does God let them grow together? Why doesn't God intervene and fix it now? It is because God created us in his own image. God made us people with intelligence and free will. And God respects our freedom. Evil comes from free choices, that is, when we choose to hurt rather than heal, and when we choose to take care of self at the expense of others. All kinds of evil result: wars, starvation, and loss of human rights and dignity. All of this comes from people freely choosing evil rather than good.

If God were to intervene to fix it now, there is only one way for God to do it, take away our free will. Then we could no longer choose evil. Then we would be programmed to always choose good. Hey, at first glance that might look pretty good, but already we can see a problem with it. If we are no longer free, we are no longer human. We have become like programmed robots. But the biggest problem is that there would be no love in the world. Love must be freely given and expressed. Love cannot be forced or programmed. If we are not free to love, the whole message of Jesus is meaningless.

Our parable teaches us that God is more patient with evil than we are. God is more patient to give us time to repent of our own bad choices, time to grow in love. Oh yes, at harvest time we will be fully responsible for the choices we have made. But in the meantime, God gives us time, encouraging us to use our freedom to choose all the good we can.

One thought I take from this parable: the awesome power to make free choices. Just as evil comes from free choice, so does goodness. Everyday we make our world better or worse by the choices we make. Let's choose all the good we can.

📖 Seventeenth Sunday of the Year
(1 Kgs 3:5, 7-12; Rom 8:28-30; Mt 13:44-46)

In our first reading God said to Solomon, "Ask something of me and I will give it to you." Wow! What an open-ended offer. Ask for anything and I will give it to you? Can we imagine that? So Solomon said, "Give me an understanding heart to judge your people and to distinguish between right and wrong." God was pleased and said to Solomon, "I give you a heart so wise and understanding there will never be anyone to equal you." Hence we have the phrase, "The wisdom of Solomon."

Now use your imagination. God says to you, "Ask anything of me and I will give it to you." You ask, Anything, Lord? "Yes, anything you ask for is yours. No restrictions. The sky's the limit." Oh boy, isn't this fun? Take a few moments to decide what you will ask for.

"Lord, make me the most beautiful and attractive person in the world. Lord, give me power and influence so people will look up to me and treat me with great esteem.

Lord, give a long and healthy life. I want to feel good for at least 100 years. Lord, I don't need to be the richest person in the world, but give me lots of money so I can afford anything I want."

Take a few moments now to finalize your request. This is it. This is your one shot to have anything you want. Don't think you have to be religious about this. Be as real as you can.

Okay, you know what your request is. Is the Lord pleased with your request? God knows human nature so well. Even Solomon surprised God a little because he asked for wisdom, not for a long life or for more riches, or for the life of his enemies. God almost expected Solomon to ask for one of these.

Another good example of our human nature is portrayed by Tevye in the Fiddler on the Roof. Tevye was not invited like Solomon to place his request before the Most High, but he did anyway since he and the Most High were old friends. His request was not to be wise, but to be rich. "If I were rich," he muses, "people would think I am wise too. They would ask my opinion, bowing, scraping because I am rich. Riches confer a certain importance and appearance of knowledge. So Lord, make me rich." Are we more like Solomon or Tevye?

In our gospel Jesus gives us the most valuable thing we could ask for. "The kingdom of heaven is like a treasure buried in a field and the person sells all he has and buys that field. The kingdom of heaven is like a pearl of great price which the merchant sells all he has to buy." The message of our gospel is starkly clear. The kingdom of heaven is the most valuable thing in our lives. Nothing else comes close. God is worth more than everything we have and are. Nothing and no one must ever take precedence over God.

And we believe that, don't we? I honestly think we all are intellectually convinced that God is most important in our lives. So our problem is not that we don't believe. Our problem is that God can seem so distant and so far off, sort of vague, not as real as all those real people and things we are dealing with every day. So people and things that are more real to us get our attention and they deserve our attention.

What can we take from today's Gospel? Let's get on with our busy lives giving attention to everyone and everything we need to. But Jesus invites us to keep focused on him as we go about our everyday lives. And to remember the bigger picture of which we are a part. He asks us to make our treasure so real to us that it is never too far beneath the surface of our thoughts, and that it gives direction and purpose to our lives and keeps us on course through all the distractions and shifting winds in our lives. Our treasure will keep everything else in proper perspective. So let us stay focused on our real treasure, my friends, and one day it will be ours.

Eighteenth Sunday of the Year
(Is 55:1-3; Rom 8:35, 37-39; Mt 14:13-21)

The kingdom of heaven is mentioned more than 100 times in the Gospels. God's kingdom is a kingdom of justice, peace, love, and joy. When justice, peace, love, and joy reign in our hearts, God's kingdom is within us. When justice, peace, love, and joy reign in our world, then God's kingdom has come to our world, just like when we pray each time we say the Our Father, "Thy kingdom come on earth just as it is in heaven."

This great emphasis on the kingdom of heaven should be saying something important to you and me. God wants us to be kingdom people. Jesus is calling us to stretch our spiritual vision, to stretch beyond ourselves to the world around us. Immediately this raises a red flag in us. Oh, oh! Now what am I going to be asked for? I have enough trouble keeping myself in line without worrying about the world. So who wants to be stretched? Probably none of us do. When we stretch before jogging or exercise it hurts. But once we get through the initial pain we're better off than if we don't stretch. I think this is true of our spiritual lives too, and Jesus wants us to keep stretching.

I believe we have a strong tendency to make our spiritual lives very personal. We focus on ourselves and on our personal salvation. "How am I doing? How do I stand before God?" Here's where Jesus stretches us. He changes our focus from ourselves to other people, to the world around us, to make God's kingdom come on earth as in heaven.

How much do we need to be stretched? When was the last time we went to confession and thought of anything other than personal sin? When have we said, "I failed to make God's kingdom more real. I failed to make my community and world better"? Oh yes, it is more comfortable to focus on ourselves and our personal salvation.

Picture the scene in today's Gospel. Jesus and his disciples were in a deserted place. A crowd came to them, 5,000 men, not counting women and children. Some commentaries estimate the crowd was actually about 20,000 people. It was getting late. Everyone was hungry and there was no food. The disciples saw the problem. They said to Jesus, "Dismiss the crowds so they can go to the villages and get food." Now comes the crux of the Gospel message. Jesus said, "There is no need for them to go away. Give them some food yourselves."

The disciples were shocked. "Five loaves and two fish are all we have here. What are you saying, Jesus?" Just imagine you had five loaves of bread and two fish in your house and there were 20,000 hungry people lined up at your door needing to be fed. How would you feel? Just like those disciples. They were paralyzed by the enormity of the situation. They reacted just like we do in the face of the enormous problems in our world around us. We don't have what it takes to do anything about this. It's all too big for us to tackle. Jesus understood but did not back down. "Bring the five loaves and two fish here to me." Bring me what you have, as meager as it seems, and together we will deal with this situation. And we know what happened, but Jesus did not do it without the meager resources of his disciples.

What is the message to us? We don't have to change the world overnight. Just give me what you have. I need what you have to make God's kingdom more real in our world. Each one of us has his or her five loaves. It may not seem like much, but Jesus needs them. Bring them to me. That's all the Lord is asking so he can do big things.

If we give our five loaves to Jesus, we don't have to worry about our personal salvation. Remember, Jesus' scene of Judgment Day: "Come you blessed people into the kingdom prepared for you by my Father because you took care of me in my need." The blessed people were surprised and asked, "Who, me? When did we take care of you?" "As long as you did it for the least of my people, you did it for me. So come on into heaven. We've been waiting for you." May we hear these same words.

📖 NINETEENTH SUNDAY OF THE YEAR
(1 Kgs 14:9a,11-13a; Rom 9:1-5; Mt 14:22-33)

Our whole relationship with God is based on faith. Today's Gospel is about faith, but before we get into it, let's looks at the characters it presents to us. Peter and his companions were fishermen. They were men of the sea. They knew when the sea was friendly and when it was treacherous. Peter did not need advice on water safety.

Some of us have had scary times in the water. I remember once I was floating on an air mattress in the Pacific Ocean, just lying there with my eyes closed, soaking up the sun. After a while I opened my eyes and was shocked to see that I had drifted out a few hundred yards from the beach. Just as I was thinking that I had to paddle back quickly, I was caught up in a huge swell and the ocean came crashing down on me. I was being tossed around under water and I didn't even know which way was up. That scary experience taught me some respect for the power of the sea.

Now picture the scene in today's Gospel. Peter and the disciples were in their boat a few miles out at sea. It was a treacherous, stormy night with high winds. The boat was being tossed about by the waves. During the fourth watch (about 3 a.m.), Peter saw Jesus walking on the sea. Impetuous Peter did it again. "Lord, if it is really you, tell me to come to you across the water." "Come," Jesus said. So Peter stepped out of the boat and began to walk on the water. Very quickly Peter came back to his senses. He realized what danger he was in. He was thinking, "My God, what am I doing out here?" He began to sink and cried for help.

Jesus rescued Peter. But hear what Jesus says to him. "What little faith you have. Why did you falter?" How little faith you have? I think Peter had great faith to get as far as he did. Would you step out of a boat onto a raging sea? I don't think I would.

What kind of faith is Jesus asking of Peter and of you and me? Our word "faith" comes from the Latin word *fides,* which means trust, confidence, reliance. The word "trust" is much stronger than the word "faith." Even Webster defines faith as complete confidence. Jesus asked Peter for such complete trust that he would step out of a boat and walk on stormy water.

Jesus asks you and me for the same absolute and complete trust, especially when things get stormy around us. Jesus asks that we trust God completely. He asks that we believe that we are part of something much bigger and more beautiful than ourselves, and that God loves and cares for us even when it does not feel like he does. He wants us to believe that there is a purpose and meaning in everything that happens to us, even what appears to be meaningless and capricious.

So who of us has faith? Who of us has complete, absolute, unshakable trust in God? That's a different question, isn't it? That's the question we need to consider and pray about.

📖 Twentieth Sunday of the Year
(Is 96:1, 6-7; Rom 11:13-15, 24-32; Mt 15:21-28)

Our gospel today is about the "in" group and the "out" group. When I was in high school, members of the T-Club were the "in" group. They had lettered in sports and they would strut down the hall in their red sweaters. They had the prettiest girls. If I sound jealous it is because I did not letter in sports. Sure, that was high school. But there is still something attractive about the "in" group isn't there? We would rather be in than out.

God's word today is about the religious "ins and outs." For 2,000 years God dealt in a special way with the Israelites, his chosen people. "You will be my people. I will be your God." And that was understandable because in a world of numerous pagan gods the Israelites held on to the truth that there is but one God. But being the way we are, wanting to be in the in group, the Israelites became rather possessive of their God. They did not want to share their God. Remember, Paul had to convince Peter that Jesus should be preached to the Gentiles, not reserved exclusively for the Jews. In today's gospel we see Jesus himself convinced that his primary mission was to the House of Israel, which made sense that the chosen people be first to hear the good news.

In our Gospel we have a classic confrontation of an insider with an outsider. Jesus, the son of David, meets a Canaanite woman. How far out was she? This is the only place in the New Testament that the word "Canaanite" is used. Matthew makes his point clear. The word Canaanite evokes all of the hateful feeling of the Jews over one thousand years. There was a long-standing tradition that the Canaanites were a sinful race that embodied all that is evil and godless. It was a race that should be exterminated. The Jews referred to them as dogs. So this woman is not only on the outs, she is as far out as she can get.

Now comes a curious part to our Gospel and a curious conversation. First of all, what was Jesus doing in Tyre and Sidon, which was Canaanite territory? Well, we could say that he either got lost or he was setting up an important teaching moment. Well Jesus did not get lost. The curious conversation went something like this. The Canaanite woman says to Jesus, "Son of David, have pity on me." Calling Jesus Son of David was itself an act of faith in him. The disciples told Jesus, "Send her away for she keeps calling out after us." Jesus says, "I was sent only to the lost sheep of the House of Israel." She pleads, "Lord, help me." Jesus replies, "It is not right to take the food of the children and throw it to the dogs." Jesus was not directing his words to the woman as much as to his disciples who needed to learn something from this. Again she asks, "Please Lord, for even the dogs eat the scraps that fall from the table of their masters." Then Jesus proclaims, "Oh woman, great is your faith! Let it be done to you as you wish."

What had Jesus done? He had cured the woman's daughter. What had he said? He had proclaimed her great faith. In the presence of his disciples, Jesus had made the outsider an insider. He responded to faith wherever he found it.

The lesson for us is that no one has a special claim on God. God is open to everyone. We used to think that because we were Catholics we were the in group. We believed that we had a head start on others getting into heaven. Because we go to church does that mean that we have more faith than those who don't? To the extent that we think we are the in group, we automatically put others out. Who do we put out? Do we put out drug dealers, prostitutes, gay people, and terrorists? Let's not forget that Jesus told us that streetwalkers, prostitutes, and tax collectors might just be the first ones into heaven ahead of you and me.

With God there is no in group and no out group. Anyone can be saved because God loves us so much that he saves us even though we have no claim on him. Let us look upon everyone as the beloved of God.

📖 Twenty-First Sunday of the Year
(Is 22:19-26; Rom 11:33-36; Mt 16:13-20)

"Who do you say I am," Jesus asked his disciples. This is the only time in the Gospels that Jesus asks directly, "What do people think of me, what do you think of me?"

What do you think of Jesus? What do I think of Jesus? Do we know for sure? Could it be that we have heard so much about Jesus that we have been programmed to think of Jesus in certain ways? Could it be that we are not even sure how we really think about Jesus?

If Jesus asked you today, "What do you think of me?" would your answer be something out of a catechism or other book? Would it be something you heard someone else say or could you answer from your own heart?

We go through life calling ourselves Christians and we are constantly addressing Jesus in prayers and receiving him in Holy Eucharist. When we die we are going to look Jesus right in the eye. Don't you think it's about time we know what we think of him?

Forget the catechisms and the books. Forget what you have

heard about Jesus. I suggest to you a way to discover what you really think of Jesus in your heart. The way we think of someone determines the way we communicate with that person. For example, if we think a person is hypersensitive and ready to explode, we tip-toe around that person like we were walking on eggs. If we think a person is understanding and sensitive and a good listener, we speak openly about ourselves. If we think a person is angry with us, we probably try to avoid the person and, if we can't, we measure our words very carefully. If we think a person likes us a lot, even loves us and really cares about us, we love to communicate with this person. We can say anything; we can share our deepest thoughts and feelings because we know we will be accepted. It's a real joy to spend time with this person every chance we get.

What we think of a person determines how we communicate with that person. So, do you want to know what you think of Jesus in your heart? Are you sure you want to know? Then look at your prayer. However we may define prayer, it is basic communication. Do you even want to pray? If you do, how do you pray?

A friend told me recently, "I can't pray anymore. I'm so angry and frustrated with God."

"Who do you say I am?" Am I a God who wishes to hear only

words of sweetness and light? Am I a person who cannot deal with the truth, who cannot handle negative feelings and anger? Am I a person who does not want you to speak with me if you are angry at me, a person who prefers silence to honesty?

"Who do you say I am?" The one thing we demand in our communication is honesty. We can't stand someone who is putting us on. We can't stand insincerity, someone who does not mean what he says.

How about our God? Does he not expect the same from us? Good prayer is honest prayer. A person who prays, "Lord, I am angry with you. I don't understand you. I'm tired of the way you are neglecting me," prays honestly and well.

I spoke recently to someone who was praying for the health of a mutual friend. I told her that the reports were positive, that her prayers were working. She said, "Oh, not mine. Lots of people are praying. It's their prayers, not mine."

"Who do you say I am?" Am I someone who listens to others but not to you? Am I a Lord who really loves other people but does not really love you?

I think it's terribly important to examine how we pray because it will tell us what we think of Jesus. And even more basic, if we pray at all or very seldom, or have no desire to pray, that too tells us what we think of Jesus.

"Who do you say I am?"

📖 Twenty-Second Sunday of the Year
(Jer 20:7-9; Rom 12:1-2; Mt 16:21-27)

Jesus began to show his disciples that he must suffer greatly and be killed. Peter took Jesus aside and said, "God forbid. No such thing shall ever happen to you." Jesus turned to Peter and said, "Get behind me, Satan!"

Get behind me Satan? Just last week Jesus called Peter "blessed," and made him head of his apostles. Now he calls him Satan. Why? Because Peter was thinking not as God does, but as human beings do. Peter still wanted Jesus to be the powerful Messiah who would lead Israel to glory. Suffering and death did not fit that picture. It was out of the question. This was Peter thinking as the human being he was.

So what was God thinking? God knew that through the suffering and death of his son the world would be saved. Heaven would be opened to everyone who wanted it. God knew that Jesus' painful and humiliating death was not the shameful end of everything that it appeared to be, but instead was the glorious beginning of a new era in our salvation history. God and Peter were on two completely different pages. They could not be farther apart. Why? Because Peter was thinking not as God does but as human beings do.

How can we know what God thinks? We find God's thoughts in God's words in scripture. Scripture is the ultimate norm we must test our thoughts against. Today's gospel gives us a few of God's thoughts to test our own against.

1. Suffering in our lives. "Whoever wishes to come after me must pick up his cross and follow me." Quite naturally, we avoid suffering every way we can. But does God see suffering differently than we do? God does not want us to suffer just to suffer. But when suffering comes anyway, does God see something in it we are missing, something saving, something redeeming just as God saw Jesus' suffering?

2. "Whoever wishes to save his life will lose it, but whoever loses his life will find it. Another gospel paradox. As we see it, it should just not be that way. The more we take care of ourselves, the more we seek our own welfare and happiness, the happier we should be. Can it be that when we lose our life, when our focus is moved from self to others, when we are more concerned with others than with ourselves, we actually find our life?

3. "What profit would there be for one to gain the whole world and forfeit his life?" What are we trying to gain in

our lives? What are we really after? Does God agree with our plans and goals or are we pursuing short-term gains and forfeiting something more valuable?

These are a few examples of how we can discover how God thinks and of how we can test our own thoughts against God's. I know how difficult this can be for us. Everything about our world is so real and God can seem so distant. Everything we grasp promises happiness and pleasure and God's promises seem so distant. It is difficult because faith and trust do not come easy. It is hard to believe that God knows best when we can't see it and to trust God when everything inside of us says no.

I am reminded of an image that might be helpful. Picture a huge tapestry. We are looking at the back side of it. What do we see? We see a lot of knots, threads and loose ends that don't seem to make sense. What in the world is this all about? This is sort of like our lives sometimes. But when we cross to the other side, suddenly we see what all those knots, threads, and loose ends add up to. We see a glorious scene, it is the scene of our lives where everything that happened to us produces a masterpiece which only God can create because God thinks as he does.

Twenty-Third Sunday of the Year
(Ez 33:7-9; Rom 13:8-10; Mt 18:15-20)

Prayer is important. Jesus said, "Amen, I say to you, if two of you agree on earth about anything about which they are to pray, it shall be granted to them by my heavenly Father." Now that sounds like a magical formula. Just find another person to pray with you for the same thing and Jesus guarantees you will get it.

Jesus is certainly talking about the power of prayer but he is not giving us a magical formula. We do not deal with God with magic. We do not force God or trick God into answering us. Throughout the Gospels Jesus has assured us that God does hear our prayer. So why don't we always get what we pray for? Jesus said; ask for anything, it shall be granted to you. Common sense tells us that God will give us anything provided it is for our good.

Is this a cop-out? Are we just giving God a way out? No, it's just plain common sense. The problem is not with God, it is with us. Sometimes we do not know what is good for us. Sometimes we don't see the big picture that God sees.

Sometimes we may feel that our prayer is no good. We get distracted when we pray. If only we could concentrate more when we pray, we say, our prayer would be so much more effective. The truth is that we are no more distracted when we pray than at any other time. Our human condition allows us only a very short span of attention, probably no more than a few seconds, before our attention is interrupted by another thought or image.

In the Middle Ages there was a monk who was following a path through the forest when he encountered a knight riding a beautiful horse. The knight saw the monk admiring the horse and said to him, "Friar, if you can say the Lord's Prayer once without being distracted I will give you my horse." The monk closed his eyes and prayed, "Our Father, hallowed…do I get the saddle too?" God knows our human condition better than we do. Don't worry about distractions, they will always be there and they do not ruin our prayer.

How many of us feel that we need to pray more than we do? Jesus said, "In your prayer do not rattle like the pagans. They think they win a hearing by shear multiplication of words. Do not imitate them. Your Father knows what you need before you ask him." So the issue is not so much how much we pray but how we pray.

We can pray in one of two ways, with faith or without faith.

We can pray without real faith, without trust or confidence that God really hears us. If this is how we pray, we don't really expect anything from our prayer. We use prayer as a last resort. You know, I've tried everything else so all I can do now is pray. If our prayer is answered we are surprised

We can also pray with real faith, with complete trust that God hears us. Now we believe Jesus. We believe that God is our loving Father that will grant us anything that is for our own good. We trust that God sees the bigger picture, that he knows better than we do, but we firmly believe that every prayer we utter is heard. As we grow in that faith and trust, we take prayer more seriously. In fact, we become careful what we pray for because we believe we will be answered. That's the kind of prayer that takes God seriously. That's the kind of prayer that God responds to. If that is our prayer, then expect that anything will happen because the question is not, does God really hear us, but rather what kind of pray-ers are we?

📖 Twenty-Fourth Sunday of the Year
(Sir 27:30-28:9; Rom 14:7-9; Mt 18:21-35)

Our Gospel today is about forgiveness, wholehearted forgiveness. This is a difficult proposition. Anyone who says it's easy to forgive has never really been hurt. Our Gospel is more than about forgiveness. It's about wholeheartedness in all of our responses to Jesus.

A guy sets up his buddy, Mark, on a blind date with a friend of a friend. But Mark has been burned before and is not too crazy about going out with someone he's never met. He protests, "What do I do if she's really ugly? I'll be stuck with her all evening." "No problem," his friend reassures him, "all you have to do is go to her door and meet her. If you like what you see, terrific, if you don't, just double over and moan 'aauugghh,' and pretend you're having an asthma attack. Then you can gracefully get out of the date without hurting her feelings." It seemed reasonable so Mark arrives at her door and rings the bell. When the young woman opens the door Mark is awestruck by her beauty and grace. Mark is about to introduce himself when suddenly she doubles over and moans, "Aauugghh."

Now you might ask, what does this story have to do with forgiveness? I think a lot. It calls the Mark in all of us to change our perspective from focusing only on ourselves as subject to hurt. There are two real people in the story. It also calls us to realize that we too need forgiveness because we hurt others probably as much as they hurt us.

Forgiveness has always been hard for people. Why else would Peter be asking Jesus, "How often must I forgive?" (Note the word "must.") Peter is not asking what he needs to do to be a really good person. He is asking for the minimum that he is obliged to do to stay out of trouble. The rabbis taught that forgiving three times was required by law. Peter is feeling pretty expansive when he suggests, "as many as seven times?" Can we imagine how he felt when Jesus answered, "Not seven times, but seventy-seven times."

Jesus is asking for unlimited, wholehearted forgiveness. That's right. We keep forgiving as often as we need to forgive. Now this should not surprise us because Jesus consistently asked for a wholehearted response. But what does "wholehearted" mean?

From the Gospels, wholehearted love means loving not just our friends, but even our enemies. It means loving God so much that we would sell everything we have to obtain his kingdom. Wholehearted faith means believing and trusting so strongly that we can move mountains or walk on water.

Has Jesus ever asked for a minimum response? He always asks for wholehearted response because Jesus wants us to be our very best. But this sounds almost impossible. But before we double over and go "aauugghh," let's reflect on this a little more.

Is Jesus asking us for more than we ask of each other? If a young couple is engaged and the bride-to-be asks her loved one, "Do you love me with your whole heart?" And he answers, "Almost, but not quite," I doubt there will be a wedding. If a wife asks her husband, "Do you love me with your whole heart?" And he answers; "Now that's a good question. Let me think about that," he had better look for another place to sleep tonight. Jesus is not asking more of us that we ask of those whom we love. But we are so conscious of our shortcomings that we just know that we are going to miss the mark. We know the very best lovers among us can still be described as limping lovers. But the important thing is to stop measuring our love and response, and to stop settling for less than our best. When a loved one asks, "Do you love me with your whole heart?" We answer, "Yes I do, and please forgive me for my shortcomings."

It is the same with Jesus. He knows we are all made of clay and easily broken. But Jesus wants us to stop measuring our love, and stop settling for less. When Jesus asks us, "Do you love me with your whole heart?" he wants to hear, "Yes, Lord, I do, and please forgive my shortcomings." Jesus forgives all when we love him with our whole heart, not measured love, but wholehearted love. Jesus smiles on us as we keep limping along coming closer and closer to wholeheartedness.

📖 Twenty-Fifth Sunday of the Year
(Is 55:6-9; Phil 1:20c-24, 27a; Mt 20:1-16a)

In today's Gospel the landowner pays his laborers equally at the end of the day even though some worked all day and others only the last hour of the day. We take issue with this Gospel because it goes against our grain. It just is not fair. Those who worked just one hour should not have received the same pay as those who bore the burden and heat of the whole day.

Technically, the landowner paid them the usual daily wage which they agreed to, and he was free to pay the same to the latecomers if he wanted to. But still, it just does not seem fair. We sympathize with those who bore the day's burden and heat, don't we?

Why is it that we object so strongly to Jesus' parable? I think for some good reasons. We are not God so we do not think like God. In our first reading from Isaiah, God said, "My thoughts are not your thoughts nor are your ways my ways. As high as the heavens are above the earth, so high are my ways above your ways and my thoughts above your thoughts."

Jesus is not speaking about good management or labor relations with employees. Jesus said this parable is about the kingdom of heaven. But even if it is about heaven, we still have a problem with it. Why? It is because we live in a society based on the merit system. We can't escape it. It is in the air we breathe. We are used to earning everything. We get only what we deserve or earn. The person who works harder deserves more. So naturally we apply our merit system to getting to heaven. When we do this we fall into the trap of thinking we are earning heaven. Every prayer we say, every temptation we overcome, and every good deed we do we put on the asset side of our ledger. We hope we will have enough assets to offset everything we put on the debit side. If things balance out right, then we earned heaven.

But God said, "My thoughts are not your thoughts." Today Jesus is saying, "Don't keep books with God. Don't present God with a bill as if God owes us something. Don't ever think you can earn or merit God's love or heaven by anything you do."

The more we apply our merit system to our salvation, the more we cheapen our redemption. We reduce Jesus' death to no purpose. In Corinthians Paul says that if we are meriting our salvation, Jesus died in vain. At best, we see the death of Jesus as merely opening the door to heaven for us and we have to work our way through.

In summary, the more we believe in our own merits, the less we need Jesus. But the more we start thinking as God thinks the more we need Jesus, the more we need to be saved by Jesus, and the more we pray, "Thank you, Lord, for loving me even though I do not deserve your love." When we start thinking as God thinks, rather than being upset by this parable, we will be ecstatic with joy because this parable tells us that God loves us more than we can imagine and has saved us by the life and death and resurrection of Jesus. We are going to heaven simply because God wants us there.

We rejoice that such love is given to us and to everyone else, even the latecomers. Then we will do all the good we can because we are so loved, rather than doing good to earn God's love. Imagine standing before God on judgment day. At that moment, will you feel more secure trusting in your own merits, will you be anxious to show God how deserving of heaven you are or will you feel more secure trusting God's love for you which has saved you?

📖 Twenty-Sixth Sunday of the Year
(Ez 18:25-28; Phil 2:1-11; Mt 21:28-32)

God loves us unconditionally no matter what we do. We cannot earn that love. It is simply ours because that is the way God is. This is what we learned from Jesus in last week's Gospel. Today Jesus poses a question about two sons and asking which one did his Father's will. Then he tells the chief priests and elders, the righteous religious leaders of his day, "Amen, I say to you, tax collectors and prostitutes are entering the kingdom of heaven before you." What a thing to say to righteous people, the people who faithfully said their prayers and followed all the laws.

I think the underlying question in our Gospel is: what is there about sinners that appealed so much to Jesus, and why did he seek them out and hang out with them and feel comfortable with them? Which raises the opposite question: why did Jesus feel uncomfortable with the righteous ones and why did he get so frustrated with them? The Gospel tells us why. It all has to do with conversion of heart, real change of heart.

The father said to the second son, "Do this," and he replied, "I will not." Later he changed his mind and did what his father wanted. This reminds me of St. Augustine who was living a pretty worldly and immoral life. He heard God's call but he was not ready. "I know I need to change, Lord, but not yet, someday." Someday came and St. Augustine experienced real change of heart and became a great saint. He regretted his no's to God for so long and wrote, "Too late have I loved you, beauty so ancient and true, too late have I loved you." But it was not too late. The father asked the same of his first son. He replied, "Yes sir, whatever you say." But he never did it. He did not think he needed to. With which son do we identify? I hope the second.

It was the tax collectors and the prostitutes who said no to God, and then God called them to something better and they said no, no. But later they experienced change of heart and mind. The chief priests and elders were like the first son. They said yes to God's call, "Yes sir, whatever you say," but they did not follow that call because they saw no need to. They were doing quite well. They saw no need to change. So Jesus said to them, "When John came to you calling for conversion of heart, you did not believe him, but the tax collectors and prostitutes did. But even when you saw that, you did not change your minds and believe." Jesus loved sinners because sinners knew they needed to change. They knew they desperately needed God and opened their hearts to God's grace. Their hearts were softened.

The righteous people thought they had their lives in good order and settled for that. They were closed to God because they did not see any great need to change. Their hearts were set. With which son do we identify? I hope the second. Haven't we said no to God many times and gone our own way? But then we recognized our sin and repented and started over again. In fact, that's the story of our lives, isn't it?

No wonder the spiritual writer Fr. Frederick Faber wrote, "The best sign of spiritual growth is constant starts and new beginnings." No wonder he wrote, "The harder you throw down a ball, the higher it bounces." No wonder a member of Alcoholic Anonymous wrote, "I wish everyone could be an alcoholic for a while because only when we hit bottom do we come up better people." No wonder someone else wrote, "The stuff that great sinners are made of is the same stuff that makes great saints." And no wonder the author Sigrid Undset wrote, "If the wrongs men and women do through lust and anger cannot be atoned for, then heaven must be an empty place."

Jesus says to us, "I don't care what you have done. I don't care how low you have been. I don't care how often you have said no to our Father. All that matters to me is that you acknowledge your sin, repent of your sin, and turn back to me. Now I can work in you. You are one of the soft-hearted.

How can we refuse such graciousness? How could we settle for things the way they are? How can we stay set in our ways when we are being invited to so much more?

Twenty-Seventh Sunday of the Year
(Is 5:1-7; Phil 4:6-9; Mt 21:33-43)

Sometimes we complain about God. We say things like, "God, if you are so good, why is there so much evil around? Why don't you fix it?" This reminds me of a movie in which Woody Allen goes to heaven and then reports back to earth. "Yes, there is a God, but he's an underachiever." When we are suffering in a heavy way we say things like, "God, if you really love me so much, why do you allow this to happen to me?" It also reminds me of a very difficult time in the life of St. Theresa of Avila when she prayed, "God, if this is the way you treat your friends, no wonder you have so few."

Today the tables are turned. God has a complaint about us. In Isaiah, our first reading, and Matthew's Gospel, the vineyard represents God's people. The readings are all about God's relationship with us, his people. Isaiah tells us everything God did for his vineyard. "What more was there to do to my vineyard that I had not done?" Matthew tells us how God did everything to convince his people he loved them. He sent prophets and they were mistreated and killed. He sent his own son, but even he was not believed and was also killed.

To understand God's complaint with us we need to get in touch with our own personal experience. Think of someone you love with your whole heart. If that person doubts your love, it hurts a whole lot, doesn't it? If you have shown your love in every way you can and that person still wonders about your love, still questions your love, we hurt so much we cry out, "I have given you all that I have and all that I am. What more can I do to convince you that I love you?"

Can we understand God now? "What more was there to do to my vineyard that I have not done? What more can I do to convince you that I love you? Why do you still wonder? Why do you still doubt?"

We need to look at the big picture of our lives. We need to step back from our daily concerns and problems and look at the whole tapestry of our lives. We need to think of all the ways that God has graced us, the way God has loved us into existence, and the way God has gifted us with our minds, bodies, talents, families, and friends. God sent his own son to die for us so we can live forever in his presence. Think of all that God has saved us from. Think of the times we flirted with danger and disaster and it did not happen. Think of the wrong paths we have started down but were saved from. Think of our pain and troubled times, and even our sins, and see how God has used it all to make us the people we are today.

How have we possibly come to this day except for a God who has loved us through everything to this very day? When we look at the big picture of our lives, it is overwhelming. Each one of us is a living miracle.

"What more can I do to convince you that I love you?" Nothing more, Lord, you have done it all. We just needed to be reminded.

📖 Twenty-Eighth Sunday of the Year
(Is 25:6-10a; Phil 4:12-14, 19-20; Mt 22:1-10)

Do we believe the good news we hear week after week? Sometimes it sounds too good to be true. When the good news tells us over and over again how much God loves us, we may find it a little too much. Can God really love me that way? If we wonder about that then our Gospel today will really blow our minds. It's about the greatest invitation we will ever receive.

We are honored by invitations, aren't we? We feel honored to be invited to the wedding or birthday of a friend. How would you feel if you were invited to a state dinner at the White House? Suppose you were in Rome and part of an audience with the Holy Father. How would you feel if the Pope pulled you aside and said, "Please join me for dinner tonight." Would you accept immediately, wholeheartedly or would you say, "Thank you, your Holiness, but I already have other dinner plans." Today's Gospel is about an invitation much greater than any of these.

Let's look at the literal meaning of the Gospel. The king is God. The wedding banquet is heaven. God first invited his chosen people, the Israelites. Some refused, some were too busy. Then God opened the banquet to everyone. He went to the main roads and invited everyone he found.

Now let's apply this Gospel to ourselves. It means God is inviting us to heaven. His invitation is just as real as going to your mailbox and finding an envelope addressed to you. You open it and read, "I respectfully invite you to heaven. I request your presence with me forever. Please RSVP." Signed, God.

Does this seem too good to be true? Do we ever say to ourselves, "I just hope God closes his eyes and let's me sneak into heaven." If we feel this way we are saying that God does not really want us in heaven. If we get there it will be through the back door, like an uninvited guest crashing the party. But today Jesus is saying, "No, you are the invited guest. God really wants you there."

Do we still squirm a little with this? Do we feel like double-checking the name on the envelope in our mailbox? Do we feel that we don't deserve this? Well you're right. None of us deserve our invitation. None of us deserve the suffering and death of Jesus. But when Jesus died, the invitation list to heaven was completed and it includes your name and mine.

My friends, I am not standing here spinning some kind of

yarn to make you feel good. I try to proclaim the Gospel as truthfully as I can. Sometimes it can be very demanding, perhaps even upsetting. Sometimes it seems too good to be true. But I didn't write the Gospel, Matthew did. It is not my parable, it is from Jesus himself. This is Gospel truth.

How will we respond? Will we ignore the invitation like some did? Will we be too busy with other things to take it seriously? No. We will respond with a wholehearted, "Yes. Yes, Lord, I won't let anything get in the way. Yes, Lord, count me in. I will be there." And you know what? The day we believe the invitation is ours, the day we respond with our whole heart, will be the day we live as people on their way to heaven.

📖 Twenty-Ninth Sunday of the Year
(Is 45:1, 4-6; 1 Thes 1:1-5b; Mt 22:15-21)

There is always so much more to the Gospel than meets the eye. Look at the scene in today's Gospel. The Pharisees were trying to trap Jesus in his speech. This was the cleverest trap of all that they put to him. Why? It was because this time they came with the Herodians. The Pharisees and the Herodians hated each other. The Pharisees hated Roman domination over them. The Herodians were fiercely loyal to Rome. Strange bedfellows, but they knew what they were doing.

Have you ever been in a situation where you were asked to say something that would surely offend one group or the other?

In their unctuous, slippery, insincere way they posed their trick question. They started by saying, "Teacher, we know you are a truthful man and you teach the way of God with truth. And you are not concerned with anyone's opinion for you do not regard a person's status. Tell us, then, what is your opinion?"

Oh boy! If anyone says that to you before asking your opinion, you know you are in trouble. Then they sprung the trap.

"Is it lawful to pay the tax to Caesar or not?" If Jesus answered yes, he would alienate the Pharisees and their large following. If he answered no, he would alienate the Herodians and would be arrested for rebellion. Did Jesus refuse to answer? No. He answered, "Repay to Caesar what belongs to Caesar," but he did not stop there, "and repay to God what belongs to God." Jesus went beyond the political question to a whole new dimension.

Let's look deeper into Jesus' answer. Historically we have misinterpreted it. We have used it as justification for separation of church and state. We believe in the separation of church and state but that is not what our Gospel is about. Even more dangerously, we have used it to divide our lives into two worlds. We separate the secular world from the spiritual world. When we do this we are living two lives: our spiritual life which belongs to God and our ordinary, worldly life which actually consumes most of our life.

This is disastrous. We limit our spiritual life to going to Mass, saying grace before meals, and, if we're lucky, maybe we find a few more moments for prayers during the day. No wonder we don't feel very spiritual. We are giving very little of our lives to God. No wonder we say things like, "I don't have time to pray. Just managing all the details of my life takes most of my time." No wonder we feel like we are trapped in a worldly life. I guess the only way to be spiritual is to go off to a monastery and run away from this worldly life of mine. Run away from our worldly life? What a disaster that would be because we would be running away from our spiritual life. We would be running away from the life that leads to holiness.

Repay to God what belongs to God. The Gospel is not one of separation, but of wholeness. Our whole life belongs to God. Certainly we need to take time to pray, but our prayers are not limited to praying times. Jesus spent most of his life working as a carpenter. Mary spent her life cooking and cleaning the house and mending socks. Were their lives worldly and secular lives?

When a father goes back to his job to support his family, is this not love? Is this not spiritual? When a mother asks herself that unending question, "What will I give them for dinner tonight?" is this not an act of love? Is this not spiritual?

Repay to God what belongs to God. Our whole life belongs to God, which means everything we do can be spiritual if we think wholeness, not separation. Let's remember that our spiritual life does not stop when we leave church.

📖 Thirtieth Sunday of the Year
(Ex 22:20-26; 1 Thes 1:5c-10; Mt 22:34-40)

It seems that life has become very complicated. One of our favorite areas to complicate is our religion.

I remember back in the seminary our basic book for spiritual formation was about 700 pages long. It seemed that becoming holy was logistically like planning the invasion of Normandy.

Why do we have 100 different novenas? Is it in case the last one did not work? I was taught that making the nine first Fridays was a sure ticket to heaven. How many times did I make them just in case?

Complicating religion is not a recent phenomenon. This is what Jesus deals with in today's Gospel. The Pharisees were still trying to trap Jesus. "Teacher, which commandment in the law is the greatest?" That sounds simple and direct. If they were talking about the Ten Commandments, any answer had a 10% chance of being right. But they were talking about the commandments in their law, which is something else. Their law had 613 commandments: 248 positive dos and 365 don'ts, one for each day of the year. Do you see how the Pharisees complicated their religion?

But again Jesus rose above their trap. "You shall love the Lord your God with all your heart, with all your soul, and with all your mind," Jesus answered, "and you shall love your neighbor as yourself." Jesus told them that the whole law, all 613 of them, depended on these two. Do you see how Jesus simplified our religion? He went from 613 to two, but he did even more than that. He reduced the law from 613 to one because Jesus made the commandment to love God and the commandment to love our neighbor the same law. These are not two loves, one going up and one going out. It is one circle of love embracing God and our neighbor.

We cannot love God and not love people. Our love of people shows our love for God. John said it bluntly in his first letter, "Those who say 'I love God' but do not love their brothers and sisters are liars. One who has no love for the brother and sister he has seen cannot love the God he has not seen" (1Jn 4:20).

Oh how simple Jesus made our religion. But we still like to complicate things. Like the Pharisees, we have made the one commandment of love very complicated. What is love? Who is my neighbor? Can I love someone I don't like? Can I love a person at the same time that I hate what the person does? On and on we go. We could fill a warehouse with books trying to explain love. God must have a great sense of humor when he sees what we have done with his simple commandment.

Jesus is asking the utmost from us. He asks for wholehearted love. We will be working at this for as long as we live. And we will always be imperfect lovers. And God understands this. But because love is difficult, we tend to look elsewhere for our spirituality. We substitute for love: prayers, self-discipline, and various religious practices. All those things are good, but they are the means to the end, they are means to make us more loving people

We need to stop looking for other ways. We need to stay focused on God's one commandment of love. We need to stop analyzing it and just do it. Life may be complicated, but let's keep our religion simple.

📖 Thirty-First Sunday of the Year
(Mal 1:14-2:2b, 8-10; 1 Thes 2:7b-9,13; Mt 23:1-12)

Our Gospel today is about being important. In our Gospel Jesus condemns the Pharisees, not because they were important people, but because they wanted to be recognized as important, and because they loved to be singled out as special and superior to other people. All their works were performed in order to be seen.

The Pharisees widened their phylacteries and lengthened their tassels. A phylactery was a small leather box that contained a few words of the Law of Moses. They wore it on their foreheads with a strap around the head. They did this so they could say that the Holy Law was always before their eyes. "See how holy we are? See how superior and important we are?" They loved places of honor at banquets, and to be greeted in the marketplace with the salutation, Rabbi. They relished in every sign of respect and importance.

Jesus said, "Do not follow their example." Think of a time when you were singled out in some way with a sign of respect. It felt good, didn't it? It was easy to accept even with humility. Now think of a time you were overlooked or ignored. It felt bad, didn't it? "I should not have been slighted like that," we might have said, "I deserve more respect than that." Our need to be important just comes as part of our wounded human nature.

A newly-appointed Army major was in his new office when a private appeared at the door. To impress the private the major said, "Come in, soldier. Be right with you after I take this phone call. Well, general, good to hear your voice. How can I help you? Fine, general, I'll call the president within the hour." Hanging up, he said to the private who was staring at the floor nervously. "Now, soldier, what can I do for you?" Without looking up the private said, "The sergeant sent me over to hook up your phone." Oh, this human nature of ours.

Jesus seems to go to the other extreme, "The greatest among you must be your servant." Is Jesus saying that God sees people very differently than we do? Are the little people really the big people in the eyes of God? Perhaps they are. Is Jesus saying that the waitress who serves might be greater than those who are served? That the house cleaner might be greater than the house owner? Perhaps he is. Is Jesus saying, "Don't be important"? No. Jesus is saying that each of us is terribly important. He is saying that he doesn't care how you are dressed, what you do, how influential you are, because each of you is terribly important, and he wants you to see yourself as important for the right reasons.

Why are you important? It is because God loves you. Can you imagine treating someone God loves so much as an unimportant person? You are important because Jesus saved you. Can you imagine treating as unimportant someone Jesus sees as so valuable that he is worth dying for? You are important because you are destined to live with God forever. Can you imagine treating a person God wants in his presence forever with anything less than utmost respect?

Jesus is saying, "Know why you are important people. See yourself as important. See each other as important." If we reflect on this we won't need anyone to explain what Jesus meant when he said, "The greatest among you must be your servant," because service comes with respect for others.

You are important. That's the truth. Thanks be to God.

📖 Thirty-Second Sunday of the Year
(Wis 6:12-16; 1 Tes 4:13-18; Mt 25:1-3)

"The kingdom of heaven is like..." This is how Jesus begins his parable in today's Gospel. He taught in parables because we remember stories and the point they make. Today's Gospel is about being ready for the kingdom of heaven at any time. Since we do not know the day or the hour, it is as if Jesus is saying, "Ready or not, here I come." But Jesus wants us to be ready. He offers us this parable to help us understand.

Picture the scene in the Gospel of an ancient Jewish wedding. The symbolic act of marriage was a solemn procession when the groom took his bride from her house to his house. This procession was held at night and the couple was accompanied by bridesmaids with torches and lanterns. The ten virgins were the ten bridesmaids who were supposed to walk with the bride and groom. What an honor! Can you feel the excitement and anticipation? But five of them were not ready. They missed the whole wedding. They were not ready.

There is a true story that is told about St. Charles Borromeo which fits this Gospel so well. When he was in the seminary he was playing chess once with a few fellow seminarians during a recreation period. One of his classmates came up with this question, "What would you do if it was revealed to you that you had one hour to live?" One of the seminarians said he would go to chapel and pray like he'd never prayed before. Another said that he would find a priest, make a general confession of his whole life and receive communion. "And you, Charles?" asked his classmate. Charles answered, "I would just continue playing chess." In other words, he believed he was always ready.

Are we ready or do we identify with the person who never seems quite ready? His wife calls to him, "It's time to go, dear." He answers, "I'm not quite ready." A friend asks him, "Will you do this?" He answers, "Oh, I'm not ready for that." A counselor asks him, "When will you stop that?" He answers, "I'm not ready yet." It is probable that when the Lord taps this person on the shoulder and says, "I have come for you," he will answer, "Oh, I'm not quite ready, Lord, could you give me a little more time?"

Time for what? Whether it's an hour or 20 years, what do we want more time for? That's the key question. If we don't know why we are not ready, we won't do anything about getting ready. So I propose a few questions which might help us to focus more. What kind of person do I want to be when the Lord comes for me? What is the difference between the person I am now and the person I want to be? What is still unresolved in my life, what is undeveloped or unfinished? What have I not yet done that I want to have done when the Lord comes for me?

Our Gospel today is not about scaring us. It's a call to do now what we need to do to become our very best. A community college professor did an exercise with his students. "Imagine," he told them, "that you are celebrating your 70th birthday. Evaluate your life. What have you done? How do you feel about it?" Some of the students said that as they looked back on their lives they would have watched more television, read more newspapers, and would have done the same things over and over. The professor was dismayed that some felt they had lived insignificant lives. God does not want that to happen to us. He wants us to get beyond the routine things of our lives and to become the people he wants us to be and who we want to be. So when Jesus says, "Ready or not, here I come," we can joyfully say, "Good to see you, Lord, I'm ready.

📖 Thirty-Third Sunday of the Year
(Prov 31:10-13, 19-20, 30-31; 1 Thes 5:1-6; Mt 25:14-38)

What kind of people are we? Are we concerned mainly with our own safety and security? Are we the kind of people who take no chances or risks, and who never step out of our comfortable, safe place? Or, are we people who are willing to take risks, to step beyond our comfort zone into new and uncharted waters? That is a crucial question because the answer tells us how we approach life itself and how we approach our spiritual lives.

In today's parable God gave differently to each servant as God has endowed us with different gifts. For example, my brother can do anything with machines. He can tear down a car into a thousand pieces and rebuild it into a new one. All I know about a car is how to drive it. But I stand before you each week proclaiming the Good News. I'm not saying that I find this easy, but you could not pay my brother any amount of money to do this.

God has endowed each of us in different ways and in different degrees. The point is, we are all gifted by God. It is not what you have that is important. It is what you do with what you have. As UCLA Coach John Wooden put it, "Do not let what you can't do interfere with what you can do."

So when the master in the parable returned to settle accounts, he found two different kinds of servants. He praised those servants who used their resources well, who took risks and produced more. He condemned the servant who, out of fear, took no risk and instead buried his talent in the ground.

What kind of servants are we? How we answer that question determines how we approach all facets of our lives. But today we focus on our spiritual lives. Are we limiting ourselves to our spiritual comfort zone? What does this zone look like? Perhaps our spiritual life is neat and predictable. Perhaps our prayers and practices are familiar ones. Maybe our good deeds are nice things we do for others which makes us feel warm inside. Maybe we love God and each other within accepted norms. We are probably looked upon by others as good and proper people.

So what's wrong with that? It sounds pretty good, doesn't it? What's wrong with it? Look at the saints. They became holy because they stepped beyond and took enormous risks. Look at God the Holy Spirit who is described as fire and rushing wind, full of surprise and wonder. Look at Jesus. If Jesus did not risk everything, where would we be today?

What's wrong with our comfort zone? I know a pastor who

refuses to try anything new until it's proven successful beyond a doubt. But since nothing can succeed unless it's tried, nothing new happens in that parish. I know a bishop who refused to take a public stand on issues because he did not have all the facts. But since he could never have all the facts, he never took a stand.

Even though our church teaches that the one law we must follow is the law written in our hearts, I know a man who knows in his heart what is right but cannot follow his conscience because it is somewhat outside the law and policy of the institutional Church. It is cold and lonely out there when we act according to our conscience. It is much more comfortable to act with institutional approval.

But you know what? We all take more risks than we think. Did you feel vulnerable and at risk when you fell in love? Did you think about risk when you got married? Were you aware of the risk every time you brought a child into this uncertain world? All of the stuff in our lives that is most real, most deeply human, most spiritual, has involved risk.

God has a big investment in each one of us and he wants a return on his investment. Don't bury your gifts out of fear. Step beyond in faith and trust. Come share your master's joy.

📖 Christ the King
(Ez 34:11-12, 15-17; 1 Cor 15:20-26, 28; Mt 25:31-46)

Today we end another Church year with the feast of Christ the King. For weeks Jesus has been teaching us in parables. This last Sunday of the year he does not give us a parable but a scenario, the scene of our last judgment. What a way to end the year.

The scene Jesus paints today is so simple it is scary. There is nothing to ponder over theologically. There is nothing to debate about like which commandment is the greatest. Jesus' scene of judgment is based on one norm only, practical love of others and loving service to others. St. John of the Cross wrote, "In the evening of life we shall be examined in love." In other words, we shall not be examined on personal status or accomplishments, but on love, our love for others in need of material and spiritual help.

We probably wish our judgment would be based on more than that. If we could rewrite this scene we would probably include all the masses we have participated in, all the prayers we have said, and all the spiritual exercises we have been so faithful to for years. Do these things count, Lord?

Today Jesus answers, "All your masses and prayers are good, but they are not the norm for your judgment. They are means to the end." They are meant to make us more loving people and that, my friends, remains the only norm for our judgment. "In the evening of life we shall be examined in love."

As young priest I was really into fulfilling my daily spiritual exercises just as I had been trained to do in the seminary. One of these practices was a period of meditation before Mass. So there I was kneeling in the sanctuary at 6:30 a.m. I was quite pious in a somewhat sleepy way. Then I heard the back door of the church open and steps coming down the aisle. I kept my eyes closed to avoid distraction. The steps came closer, the communion rail opened and someone tapped me on the shoulder and asked if I would hear his confession. I admit my initial reaction was somewhat less than positive. I was thinking to myself, "How dare you interrupt my meditation? Can't you see I'm doing what a good priest is supposed to do?" But I went back to the confessional and heard his confession. By the time I got back to my kneeler, the Lord was getting his message through to me, "You are here to serve the needs of others. Sure your prayer is important, but the needs of others take precedence over your prayer." Yes, in the evening of life we shall be examined in love.

St. Paul understood this when he wrote one of the most powerful passages in the scriptures. "If I speak with human tongues and angelic as well, but do not have love, I am a noisy gong and clanging symbol. If I have the gift of prophecy and comprehend all mysteries, if I have faith great enough to move mountains, but I have not love, I am nothing." Now Paul gets really serious. "If I give away everything I have, if I hand over my body to be burned, but I have not love, I gain nothing" (1 Cor 13).

Yes, in the evening of life we shall be examined in love. Today Jesus gives us the scene of our judgment. It is so clear and perhaps scary, but we cannot rewrite it. Lord, give us the grace to keep our priorities right, the grace to live your simple commandment.